REVISED 2ND EDITION

The Waiter & Waitress and

Waitstaff Training Handbook

A Complete Guide to the Proper Steps in
Service for Food & Beverage Employees

First Edition by
Lora Arduser and Douglas Brown

Revised by
Taylor Centers

THE WAITER & WAITRESS AND WAITSTAFF TRAINING HANDBOOK: A COMPLETE GUIDE TO THE PROPER STEPS IN SERVICE FOR FOOD & BEVERAGE EMPLOYEES

Copyright © 2017 Atlantic Publishing Group, Inc.

1405 SW 6th Avenue • Ocala, Florida 34471 • Phone 800-814-1132 • Fax 352-622-1875
Website: www.atlantic-pub.com • Email: sales@atlantic-pub.com
SAN Number: 268-1250

Library of Congress Cataloging-in-Publication Data

Arduser, Lora.
 The waiter & waitress and waitstaff training handbook : a complete guide to the proper steps in service for food & beverage employees. — Revised 2nd edition.
  pages cm
 Includes bibliographical references and index.
 ISBN 978-1-62023-056-5 (alk. paper) — ISBN 1-62023-056-9 (alk. paper) 1. Table service — Handbooks, manuals, etc. 2. Waiters — In-service training — Handbooks, manuals, etc. 3. Waitresses — In-service training — Handbooks, manuals, etc. I. Brown, Douglas Robert, 1960- II. Title. III. Title: Waiter and waitress and waitstaff training handbook.
 TX925.A72 2015
 642'.6--dc23

                                                                                        2015034308

Printed in the United States

PROJECT MANAGER: Rebekah Sack • rsack@atlantic-pub.com
INTERIOR LAYOUT AND JACKET DESIGN: Nicole Sturk • nicolejonessturk@gmail.com

Reduce. Reuse.
RECYCLE.

A decade ago, Atlantic Publishing signed the Green Press Initiative. These guidelines promote environmentally friendly practices, such as using recycled stock and vegetable-based inks, avoiding waste, choosing energy-efficient resources, and promoting a no-pulping policy. We now use 100-percent recycled stock on all our books. The results: in one year, switching to post-consumer recycled stock saved 24 mature trees, 5,000 gallons of water, the equivalent of the total energy used for one home in a year, and the equivalent of the greenhouse gases from one car driven for a year.

Over the years, we have adopted a number of dogs from rescues and shelters. First there was Bear and after he passed, Ginger and Scout. Now, we have Kira, another rescue. They have brought immense joy and love not just into our lives, but into the lives of all who met them.

We want you to know a portion of the profits of this book will be donated in Bear, Ginger and Scout's memory to local animal shelters, parks, conservation organizations, and other individuals and nonprofit organizations in need of assistance.

– Douglas & Sherri Brown,
President & Vice-President of Atlantic Publishing

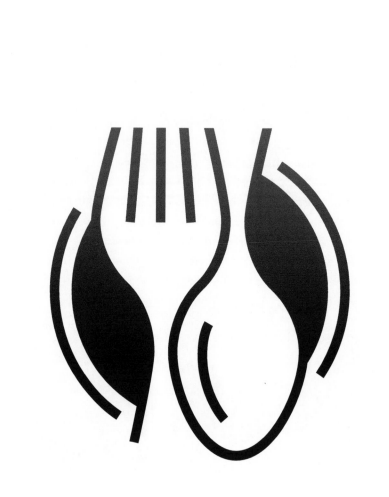

Table of Contents

Introduction 13

Chapter 1: The Serving Staff 17

How to Hire a Good Service Staff 17

What Makes a Good Server? 17

Job Lists 21

Server Job List.. 22

Bus Person Job List.. 24

Providing Great Service..26

Service – What *Not* To Do!..32

Chapter 2: Types of Service and Table Settings 35

Types of Restaurants..35

Chapter 3: Hosting 41

Duties of the Restaurant Host/Hostess.........................42

Inspecting the Dining Room 49

Providing Excellent Service 50

Supervising the Service 51

The Nature of Host Work 52

Performing Clerical Work 54

Making Arrangements for Special Parties 54

Serving Special Parties 56

Receiving Customers... 57

Chapter 4: Table Service 61

American Service... 62

French Service 62

English Service 64

Russian Service 65

Buffet Service... 65

Family-Style 66

Left or Right?... 66

Table Side Service... 68

Table Settings 73

Setting the Table... 74

General Rules for Table Service...................................... 83

Setting an Elegant Table 92

Folding Napkins 92

Centerpieces 94

Chapter 5: Taking Orders... 97

Giving and Collecting Orders 99

Approaching the Table.. 101

Giving a Friendly Greeting 102

Giving Prompt Attention.. 103

Taking a Drink Order... 103

Serving the Drinks 104

Explaining the Menu..104

Taking the Food Order 105

Delivering the Food 105

Checking Back 106

Dessert 106

Presenting the Check..106

Clearing the Table 109

Serving Multiple Tables...110

Tips for Serving Customers.. **111**

Chapter 6: Carrying Trays 119

Food Trays 120

Loading Trays 120

Cocktail Trays..121

Arm Service..121

Bussing...121

Chapter 7: Suggestions and Suggestive Selling 123

Suggesting Selections to the Customer 124

Making Substitutions...126

Purposes of Suggestive Selling 126

Suggesting Additional Items..129

Suggesting Higher-Priced Items 131

Value-Added Service 133

Chapter 8: Take Care of the Kids................................. 143

Speedy Service 144

Kid-Friendly Menus...144

Healthy Choices 144

Kids' Specials..145

Kid-Friendly Cups 145

Games and Play Spaces...145

Talk to the Kids..145

Seats 146

Keep an Eye out for Messes...147

Changing Stations 147

Step Stools...147

Chapter 9: Server Side-Work Duties **149**

Setting Up Coffee Service 152

Setting Up Bread Baskets..153

Handling Customer Complaints...153

Dealing with Difficult Customers 155

Remember These Golden Rules **157**

Handling Problems 158

Chapter 10: Menu Knowledge **165**

Cooking Terms and Methods on Preparation 167

Chapter 11: Restaurant Technology **171**

New Technology 171

Electronic Ordering..172

Handling Money 175

Writing Orders...177

Presenting the Check..177

Problems 180

Guest Tickets and the Cashier....................................181

Getting Orders to the Kitchen 184

Chapter 12: Tipped Employees 189

The Tip Rate Determination and Education Program 190

Additional Information on Tip-Reporting.......................192

Employee Tip-Reporting Frequently Asked Questions..........193

Tips-Reporting Policies...196

Chapter 13: Beverage Service 197

Alcohol Sales Policies 197

Alcohol Safety 199

How to Serve Alcohol 201

Types of Alcohol 203

Bar Terms...210

Wine...212

Bottle Sizes...213

Wine Language..214

Helping a Customer Choose Wine 214

Serving Wine...215

Pronunciation 215

Wine and Food..215

Wine Resources 215

Wine Labels...217

Tasting Tips...219

Describing Wine...220

Glassware 222

Serving Wine 222

Pouring Procedures...225

Free-Pouring...228

Pouring Draft Beer..230

Common Beer-Pouring Problems................................233

Real Whipped Cream..235

Freshly Squeezed Juices 236

Garnishes 236

Enhancing Drink Quality 237

Chapter 14: Bussing...243

Chapter 15: Sanitation and Safety 247

Red Cross...248

Fire department 248

OSHA...248

Preventing Accidents 248

Strains..250

Slipping and Falling 250

Fires...251

Choking 252

Exposure to Hazardous Chemicals 253

How to Read the MSDS 255

What is HACCP?...256

Avoid Bacterial Cross-Contamination 258

Online Information Resources.....................................260

Bacteria Primer 261

Dangerous Forms of Bacteria 264

Controlling Bacteria 266

Hygiene 267

Conclusion...**271**

Glossary **273**

Bibliography **275**

Index...**277**

Introduction

In many countries, waiting on tables is considered an honorable profession and a respectable way to earn a living. There are even schools to educate people on how to become professional servers. This is not the case in the United States. When interviewing servers to join your team, you will most likely see students, working parents, or people looking for part-time or in-between employment. And since most of these servers skipped the fancy European waiter universities, you will need to invest in training and education in order to reduce turnover and increase productivity.

Technology is important in training, but getting through to your employees is even more important. Of course, the different types of food service affects the duties assigned to waiters, but certain fundamental duties are common in all food operations.

 **Fast Fact**

In America, one in three people found their first job in a restaurant.[1]

The precise dining room procedures may differ somewhat between one food service unit and another. A waitperson's efficiency is measured by the carefulness and completeness with which his or her duties are performed — before the meal service, before the customer's order is taken, after the meal service, and after the customer has left the table.

1. The National Restaurant Organization, 2016

Numerous industry surveys show that waitstaff service is often the primary factor in a customer's decision to return to the restaurant or go to a competitor instead. Offering great food is not enough to stay competitive. It is up to you, the manager, to train, motivate, and supervise the staff to ensure that customers return and spread the word about your establishment.

This newly revised and updated training handbook was designed for all food service serving staff members. It covers every aspect of restaurant customer service from hosts and head waiters to waitresses and wine stewards. The detailed performance of each position is described for different types of establishments and service—including French, American, English, Russian, Family-Style, and Banquet. It also provides step-by-step instructions on subjects like hosting, seating guests, table-side service, service techniques, getting customers to order quickly, handling problems, promoting specials, food safety, and much more.

Chapter 1
The Serving Staff

How to Hire a Good Service Staff

The key to hiring good, competent employees is to put aside personal prejudices and select applicants only because you feel they will have a better chance of being successful at the job. Some applicants may have excellent experience but be sorry workers, and sometimes a fantastic employee will come to you without any prior server experience at all. You have to make a judgment call. Reviewing and choosing potential restaurant employees not an easy task, but this section is here to provide you with the information necessary to discover the perfect candidate.

What Makes a Good Server?

Servers are essentially the internal marketing tools of your restaurant's brand. They are the link between your customers and sales, so you want a server who is going to be successful at marketing both the menu and the establishment to your guests.

Fast Fact

More than half of all adults have worked in the food industry at some point in their lives.[2]

---

2. The National Restaurant Organization, 2016

Obviously, knowledge and experience make a person a good server, but what character traits should you look for? If you want an employee that shines, here are some qualities to look out for:

Effective communicator

One of a server's main jobs is to communicate with customers and the rest of the staff. Servers should be able to verbally communicate with a wide range of personalities—anywhere from overwhelmed chefs to moody customers. This communication extends to facial expressions and body language as well. For example, if a server is scowling at a guest, he or she is communicating negative emotions, and the customer may feel unwanted. On the other hand, a natural smile implies that the customer is welcome.

High energy

Restaurant serving is a tough job that requires long hours of walking and talking without a minute's rest. Servers need to be able to maintain a high level of positive energy throughout their shift.

Flexibility

Servers should be flexible and able to deal with sudden, unexpected rushes that require them to extend their shift. They also need to be flexible and tolerant in dealing with the public.

Can handle stress

The restaurant world is an extremely stressful one. A 2016 study out of Southern Medical University in Guangzhou, China, found that restaurant servers often endure more stress than neurosurgeons. Servers have to deal with physical and mental strain on a daily basis, which can take the form of annoying customers, a thankless kitchen crew, another server that won't pull his or her own weight, or simply dealing with the challenges of a full restaurant. Coupled with the burden of low wages, this is not an environment for the faint of heart.

Cooperative

Restaurants are like battleships. They require a good deal of teamwork, compliance, and vigilance. Therefore, all servers should be willing to pitch in and help whenever they can. For example, a good server will help the salad person when he or she is backed up; a less than ideal server will stand and think, "Eh . . . not my job."

Courteous

Servers should be polite and courteous with their managers, guests, and fellow employees. Workers are more efficient when they aren't irritated with each other, and customers are more likely to return if they are treated with respect.

Desire to please others

The job of server is aptly named. A person working in such a position should get satisfaction from pleasing other people. A server must be able to put his or her ego in check for the good of the customer (and for the good of the tip).

Empathic

Good servers can read a customer quickly to see if they want to be alone or are interested in chatting. This ability to feel and reflect another person's mood is helpful for setting the right tone for a guest. If a solitary diner is reading, the server shouldn't assume the person is lonely. If the guest encourages conversation, that's fine. Otherwise, he or she may simply be interested in the book they've brought along!

Neat appearance

Servers need to be neat and clean. Your server indicates to your guest how clean and organized your facility is. If the server runs up to the table frantically searching for a pen, wearing a dirty apron and shirt, the customer is going to feel that this reflects how much you care about the rest of your operation.

Job Lists

Before you can teach someone a job, you must be able to break that job down into discrete steps. A job list is a list of all the duties a person in a particular position must perform. These lists can help managers in hiring, training, and evaluating employees.

To develop these lists, you should break all jobs down into broad categories, such as customer service, opening duties, and kitchen duties. Then you should group tasks associated with the job under these categories. Think about every single thing you can that is associated with a particular job function when developing these lists. Remember, for someone who has never preformed the job before, no task is too small to mention. You might consider having an employee or employees help you with these lists or you might want to trail an employee while creating the lists yourself.

You'll need to make a determination of how detailed you want these lists to be. "Taking an order" may be too general of a term to use for your training list. For example, you may need to break this task down into several stages. How detailed your lists are partially depends on your establishment. If you have an extremely varied menu, your cook's job list may be very detailed and extensive, for example.

 **Fast Fact**

Jobs change over the course of time — make sure your job lists change as well!

For training purposes, you can make these lists checklists, putting a blank before each task so you can check it off as the employee masters that particular skill. These duties should be listed as specifically as possible so there is no confusion about the actual duties you want employees to perform.

A sample server and busser job checklist follows.

Server Job List

Name: _____

Reports to: _____

Hire Date: _____

Employee must be able to:

(When employee has mastered each task, please place a check mark beside the task.)

General

____ Hospitable to guests
____ Neat appearance
____ Punctual and has a good attendance record
____ Was trained in and follows correct procedures for finding subs
____ Proper way to serve alcohol responsibly
____ Tipping procedures and laws
____ Company policies including scheduling, pay, break times and sexual harassment

_____ Personal hygiene
_____ Safe food-handling
_____ Heimlich Maneuver
_____ Safe work place procedures

Service

_____ The sequence of service
_____ Greeting guests
_____ Filling drink orders
_____ Serving drinks
_____ Serving wine
_____ Suggestive selling
_____ Taking appetizer and entrée orders
_____ Serving appetizer and entrée orders
_____ Clearing table during meal service
_____ Dessert suggestion
_____ Serving dessert
_____ Presenting check
_____ Properly bussing table when service has concluded
_____ Resetting table

Side Duties

_____ Folding napkins
_____ Setting tables prior to service
_____ Stocking stations
_____ Making coffee/tea
_____ Refilling salt, pepper and condiments
_____ Refilling sugar
_____ Other _____

Closing Duties

_____ Cleaning side stations
_____ Restocking service areas
_____ Resetting tables for next shift
_____ Cleaning service trays

Handling Guest Checks

____ Knowledge of computerized cash register
____ Opening a check
____ Entering items on a check
____ Procedures for voiding checks
____ Deleting items from a check
____ Proper customer payment procedures
____ How to operate credit card machine
____ Giving back change
____ Running report at end of shift for open guests checks

Menu Knowledge

____ Description (including taste) of all menu items
____ Description of wines and how to pair wines with entrées
____ Knowledge of preparation techniques
____ Potential food allergies and customer diet concerns and alternatives

Bus Person Job List

Name: _____
Reports to: _____
Hire Date: _____

Employee must be able to:

(When employee has mastered each task, please place a check mark beside the task.)

General

____ Hospitable to guests
____ Neat appearance

_____ Punctual and has a good attendance record
_____ Was trained in and follows correct procedures for finding subs
_____ Company policies including scheduling, pay, break times, and sexual harassment
_____ Personal hygiene
_____ Safe food-handling
_____ Heimlich Maneuver
_____ Safe workplace procedures

Set-Up Duties

_____ Set up tables prior to service
_____ Rolling silverware
_____ Preparing water pitchers and water glasses
_____ Preparing bread baskets
_____ Cleaning bus pans and trays
_____ Checking restrooms for cleanliness

Service Duties

_____ Clear dishes from table in a quiet and efficient manner
_____ Set up table place setting correctly
_____ Empty trash from dining room and kitchen
_____ Make and refill coffee and tea
_____ Seat guest
_____ Know how to work the dishwashing machine
_____ Know how to put away clean dishes and kitchenware
_____ Delivering dishes to dishwasher
_____ Proper way to stack and carry dirty dishes from tables
_____ Proper way to deliver and stack clean dishes from dishwasher

Closing Duties

_____ Cleaning back kitchen
_____ Cleaning bus pans and carts
_____ Resetting tables
_____ Sweeping

Providing Great Service

Great service doesn't just happen by accident. There are many things your servers and you can do to give your customers exceptional service. Consider the following opportunities:

Smile

This is one of the simplest yet most important things servers (and the management) can do. Smiling sets the tone and sets everyone at ease; it makes the server approachable for the customer. If the staff is unsmiling and surly, customers may never return to your establishment.

Servers stay with diners

In many restaurants today, managers use multiple employees to wait on a table. While this results in speedy delivery, it can also confuse the guest. Give your servers the opportunity to connect to the guest; let them be the sole liaison between restaurant and guest. Of course, this doesn't mean that no one should help the server if he or she is behind.

Maintain a database

Keep a record of your regular customers' likes, dislikes, birthdays, anniversaries, etc. Nothing makes a customer feel more special than having his or her birthday remembered—without even prompting! Use your computer system to develop such a database or simply keep a notebook. Many restaurants have point-of-sale (POS) systems that capture information such as birthdays, anniversaries, etc. If you don't have such a system, create your own. You can capture the information though customer surveys. Give this information to the host or hostess. Include people's names and what particular guests like to drink. Also, inform servers about forthcoming special occasions.

Maintain an online presence

In today's ever-growing digital environment, having a website is more important than ever. A website allows you to provide customers with the history behind your establishment, a copy of your menu, as well as helpful information like restaurant hours, the day's specials, and directions. In addition to a website, you should also consider creating social media pages for your restaurant on platforms like Facebook and Twitter. This is a fantastic way to stay in contact with patrons, provide promotional materials, develop a mailing list for newsletters, and advertise your restaurant for free.

Recognition

Recognition is very important, but it doesn't necessarily need to be elaborate. It can be as simple as addressing the customer by name.

Listen carefully for information from customers

Better to overcommunicate than to drop the ball. Servers may want to repeat information back to customers, especially if the order is detailed. This will let the guest know the server wrote it down correctly. If your restaurant doesn't use guest checks when taking the customer's order at the table, this device can be particularly important for reassuring the customer.

Make eye contact

As a culture, Americans tend to trust people who look you in the eye. Look directly at the customer you are addressing. Give your guests your undivided attention and let them know that you are listening. Don't stare at the table, the floor or the artwork on the wall. Clear your head, smile and pay attention. Make sure you're *at* the table when you're talking. Don't talk to your guests as you're flying by; it makes people feel unimportant, and no one likes that feeling.

Use an expediter

An expediter is someone who maintains the pace in the kitchen. This person keeps track of the food coming out of the kitchen and makes sure servers know where their plates are and what needs to go out to the dining room next. This person can be key in making sure service is smooth and timely. You don't necessarily need to hire someone just for this position. If your seasoned veterans would like more hours, have them fill this position on a rotating basis.

Create shorthand codes

All restaurants use shorthand on their guest checks to communicate information. It's simply quicker than writing everything out. Make sure your servers are well acquainted with the appropriate codes. It can be disastrous if they start to make up their own!

Rules of the road

Have set traffic rules in your establishment. Make sure that aisles don't become clogged. For example, if two servers are heading for the same table, the first one should go to farthest side of the table. Always let the guest go first, then a server with food and finally the busser.

Rules of recovery

Accidents are bound to happen — how you handle the accident is the important thing. First, promptly offer an honest, sincere apology. Second, take steps to resolve the problem. Let's say one of your servers spills tomato bisque on the white shirt of one of your lunch customers. The server should immediately help clean up the customer, then the server or a manager should offer to pay for the dry cleaning. Suggest that the customer send you the bill and you can take care of it for them. If a customer's food is wrong or prepared incorrectly, immediately get the food to the guest who has had to wait immediately. To aid recovery in these situations, it might be a good idea to consider having a floater position. This person could work during the rush hours and basically wander through the restaurant ready to fix and forestall any problems.

Customer satisfaction survey

Some people are shy about telling you they've had a bad experience in your restaurant. You can still get feedback from these more reticent customers by using customer satisfaction surveys. Have the server offer these with the check. They can be self-addressed and stamped for the customer to drop in the mail later or they can fill them out and leave them at their table. You can share this feedback, good and bad, with your staff later. Use the negative feedback to improve your restaurant. Use positive feedback to give specific employees accolades for their good work.

Be courteous

Seems like common sense, but it's amazing how many servers don't treat guests with common courtesy. Make sure your servers say "Thank you" and "You're welcome." The terms "ma'am" and "sir" are often appropriate as well.

 **Fast Fact**

The majority of customers consider proper service to be the definitive factor of a good dining experience. If your servers aren't courteous, your customers aren't satisfied.

Be knowledgeable

One of the best resources your servers have for increasing their tips is to be knowledgeable about the menu. They should be able to tell a guest if the soup du jour is cream-based or if the shrimp is sautéed or grilled. Use language peppered with adjectives when describing menu items; you want to provide the customer with a mouth-watering mental image. For example, try saying, "Our special tonight is a rack of lamb, braised in a Merlot and rosemary broth and served with a savory wild mushroom bread pudding and fresh roasted asparagus." Servers should also be well informed about the establishment itself and be able to answer questions such as operating hours, which credit cards accepted and types of service available.

Acknowledge the customer quickly

Customers need to be acknowledged within 30-60 seconds of being seated. Don't leave them waiting. Waiting will negatively affect a customer's mood, and a guest's mood is highly likely to affect the tip. If a server is swamped, train your host staff and bussers to help out. Even stopping for a second and saying, "I'll be right with you," will make the customer comfortable in the knowledge that they will receive prompt, good service within seconds.

Up-selling

Up-selling will increase tips because you're increasing the total amount of the sale, and most people tip on a percentage of the total. Have servers suggest appetizers, desserts and premium drinks. Don't let them strong-arm the guest, however. For instance, if a customer orders a gin and tonic, the server could say, "Do you prefer Tanqueray, Beefeaters, or our house gin?" This simple suggestion may influence a customer to order a call brand rather than a well brand.

Resolve problems

Train your servers to resolve any problems — quickly. You also need to train the kitchen staff that problems need to be resolved immediately. If a customer gets the wrong order or if their food is not prepared as they requested, tell your servers to apologize and offer to fix the problem. The server must also notify the kitchen that the replacement meal needs to be turned round quickly. If the server is unsure how to resolve a problem, you or a manager need to be available to come up with a solution. It's also a nice gesture to give the patron a break on the check. If someone ordered a medium-rare steak and was served a rare steak, make part of the apology a free round of drinks or dessert.

Show gratitude

People are dealing with a lot in their lives and you have a chance to "make their day." Express gratitude in the tone of your voice when you thank them for their patronage. Making them feel appreciated will make them remember you — as they fill out the tip and the next time they're deciding where to eat!

Service — What *Not* To Do!

Just as there is a list of tried-and-tested procedures that make great service, there is also a list of things that inevitably lead to poor service. Make sure your servers aren't engaging in any of the following practices.

All thumbs

Clumsy servers not only look bad, but they can cause accidents. You can't enroll your servers in charm school, but you can give them tips on how to handle trays and plates.

✗ Fast Fact

To avoid hiring someone that may not have the grace required to serve tables, have applicants give a demonstration of their serving skills during the interview.

Unkempt appearance

Be sure your servers' physical appearance makes a good impression on your guests. Servers' uniforms should be neat. All employees should be well groomed and they should not smell offensive.

Attitude

Don't let your servers get away with ignoring your guests. Even though some waitstaff do the job adequately, their attitude leaves a lot to be desired. Surly servers who seem to be in a hurry or who fail to make eye contact do nothing for your guests' appetites.

Don't be intrusive

Customers want attention and service, not another person at the table. Train your waitstaff to be attentive, without being overbearing or intrusive. Servers should never get too personal with guests, nor should they engage in overly long conversations.

Chapter 2
Types of Service and Table Settings

Types of Restaurants

There are millions of restaurants in the world, and for each restaurant, there are probably three or four ways you could categorize it. Let's keep it simple, though. For our purposes, we're going to boil it down to three basic types: Fine dining, bistro/trattoria, and family.

Fine dining restaurants usually offer china and table linens in a luxurious surrounding. A host (or maître d') is in charge of captains, servers, bus people, and sommeliers (wine stewards). The menu and wine list is usually extensive, as is the bill. The pace of service in a fine dining establishment is leisurely with meals often lasting up to three hours.

The bistro/trattoria category covers a range of restaurants from white tablecloth establishments with a range of menu styles to smaller venues with simple food choices. Traditionally, bistros and trattorias were family operated, but now the term generally refers to any simple restaurant.

Family restaurants include family-style diners and theme restaurants. These restaurants usually do not have linens or fine china, the food is fairly simple, and often the staff has less experience than those at the above-mentioned types of restaurants.

All restaurants have the same basic front-of-the-house positions, but finer dining establishments will have a more extensive staff. In all three of these restaurant types, you are likely to find a general manager, dining room managers, hosts, servers, bartenders (if the restaurant serves alcohol), and bus people. In fine-dining establishments, however, you may also find a wine steward and a captain.

The general descriptions of the duties of all these positions are listed below:

General manager

The GM is responsible for the entire operation. This person is responsible for the overall management of the dining room and bar services, including facility management and public relations.

Dining room manager

This person is in charge of dining room service. Some of his or her duties include maintaining operating cost records, hiring and training front-of-the-house employees, working with serving staff to ensure quality food and beverage presentation, ensuring proper food-handling procedures, handling guest complaints, and helping to plan menus.

Captain

The person in this position is usually responsible for service in a particular section of tables. He or she may take orders and assist the servers in that section. Since the captain is ultimately responsible for the service in that section, he or she rarely leaves the floor.

Host

The host greets and seats customers, takes phone reservations and looks after the front lobby area. (In casual restaurants, this position usually takes the place of the general manager or captain.) The host or hostess will also assign service stations to all servers and bussers, inform service personnel of menu changes and daily specials, provide menus to guests, and manage special seating requests of guests consistent with table availability.

Wine Steward

This person is responsible for the creation of a wine list, maintaining the wine inventory, recommending wines to customers, and serving bottled wine.

Head waiter

This person may also be known as a maitre d'. He or she manages a restaurant's dining room to ensure that guests have a pleasant dining experience. The tasks undertaken by the head waiter include ensuring that waiters and waitresses are quick on their feet and able to answer customer enquiries on the day's dishes, ensuring dishes arrive promptly, ensuring that staff are dressed properly, organizing the wait system, and supervising the restaurant clean-up and closing duties.

Server

A server is responsible for coordinating serving stations and providing customers with quality service. His or her primary duties include: greet guests and provide them with menu information, including preparation techniques, specials and wine pairings; communicate with dining room and kitchen personnel; take food and drink orders using appropriate procedures; serve food and beverages according to standard procedures; total bill and accept payment; and stock station and perform assigned side duties.

Bus person

Bus people assist food servers to maintain service efficiency and ensure guest satisfaction by maintaining cleanliness of the front-of-the-house area. He or she greets guests appropriately when they are seated; communicates with host or hostess and waitstaff to maintain service efficiency and ensures guest satisfaction; maintains cleanliness and sanitation of the front-of-the-house including all tables, chairs, floors, windows, and restrooms; removes dirty dishes and utensils from tables between courses; clears tables after guests leave; and may assist waitstaff in serving tables with hot beverages such as coffee or tea.

Chapter 3

Hosting

While a restaurant may operate like an even-keeled battleship behind the scenes, it also needs to be warm and welcoming to the customer. Every employee in your restaurant is a host, and every customer is your guest. Generally, the host or hostess greets the customers as they enter the dining room and ushers them to tables. However, when the host is busy or the establishment does not have a host, it becomes the waitstaff's responsibility to meet and seat customers. Whether guests receive a favorable or an unfavorable impression of the restaurant depends on the manner in which this service is performed. Remember what they say, "Your first impression is your last impression."

The primary function of the host or hostess, as the name signifies, is to dispense hospitality. The hostess represents the management when he or she receives the customers. Acting as the representative of the management of the business, he or she should greet customers graciously and try to make them feel that they are welcome guests.

Upon the host or hostess rests the responsibility of giving customers the impression, as soon as they enter the restaurant, that they may expect good service. The host or hostess shares responsibility with the server for the customers' satisfaction with the service they receive. A pleasant reception, careful service throughout the meal, and courteous treatment as they leave will impress customers with the excellence of the service and make them feel that their patronage is appreciated. It is the feeling of being a valued patron that converts occasional customers into regular guests of the restaurant.

The host or hostess has working relations with all the individuals concerned with restaurant sales and service-the manager, the server and the guests. He or she, therefore, needs to be equipped by personality, ability and training for the liaison position he or she holds. The host or hostess must interpret management's policies and standards to the customers, and convey the wishes of both the management and the guests to the sales staff.

 **Fast Fact**

The skill of the host or hostess often determines the efficiency of the restaurant's service and the satisfaction of its guests.

Duties of the Restaurant Host/Hostess

The restaurant hostess has various duties to perform in connection with her relations with the customer, the servers and the restaurant management. In performing these duties, he or she plays an important part in bringing about the consistently prompt and careful kind of service that will satisfy guests.

The host or hostess represents the management to the customer; he or she conveys the wishes of both the management and the customer to the sales staff and kitchen force; and he or she reports to the management the commendation, the suggestions and the complaints of both customers and employees. Good judgment and tact on the part of the host or hostess in these relationships, therefore, are essential.

The restaurant host or hostess needs background knowledge of correct procedures in food service and a working knowledge of psychology in order to handle his or her work efficiently. He or she also should be familiar with the policies and regulations of the business. Until the host or hostess has mastered this information, he or she will not be thoroughly effective in supervising the service, dealing with customers and assisting management to execute the business policies.

In a the host or hostess's daily work, he or she should be familiar with regulations concerning the seating of customers, serving, filling orders in the kitchen and party service. In addition, there are a number of general matters on which he or she should be informed.

Policy concerning seating

- Is the customer permitted to designate that a particular waitperson shall serve him?

- Does the policy of the restaurant approve seating strangers at the same table?

- During what hours are reservations permitted? How long should tables be held?

Policy concerning serving

- What is the prescribed method for a table setup?

- What specific method of service is used for:

  - Table d'hôte meals?

- A la carte orders?

- Special parties?

- What is the division of work between the waitstaff and bus persons? What duties are each expected to perform independently? What duties are performed jointly?

- Are extra servings of hot bread offered? Are second cups of coffee allowed without extra charge?

- When and under what conditions may substitutions be made on a menu? Is there an extra charge when a guest requests a substitution?

Policy concerning filling orders in the kitchen

- What foods does each kitchen station serve?

- What is the best routine for a waitperson to use in filling an order?

- To whom at each serving station should the waitperson give the order?

- Where are supplies of dishes, glassware, silver and linen kept?

- Where may extra supplies of butter, cream, ice, crackers and condiments be found?

- Are waitstaff required to dish their own orders of desserts and ice cream?

- Are waitstaff expected to make tea and coffee and fill orders for other beverages? Exactly what directions should be followed?

- Are "outs" and substitutions on the menu posted on a board in the kitchen? Should the menu cards be changed accordingly?

Policy concerning large party service

- What special rooms and dining room spaces may be reserved?

- What is the largest number of persons that can be accommodated? What is the smallest number for which any one room may be reserved?

- Is any leeway allowed on the guaranteed number of guests? What are the specific regulations concerning this matter?

- At what hours is party service provided? How late may a group remain?

- What is the minimum price for which a special group may be served? What is the usual price?

- What provisions are made for flowers and decorations?

- Is a portable stage available for the speaker's table and for entertainers?

- Are there electrical connections, extension cords and screens available to use for the slide projector or video equipment?

- What is the policy with respect to gratuities?

- Is a special crew provided for party service? How are the members of these crews secured?

General policy

- Are guests permitted to use the dining room or office telephones?

- Are menus provided as souvenirs without charge?

- Are pies, cakes and rolls made to order? Other foods?

- Are lunches packed to order?

- Are tray meals sent out?

The service in your restaurant can make or break your operation. Numerous industry surveys show that waitstaff service is often the deciding factor in returning to a restaurant or going to a competitor instead. Offering great food is not enough to stay competitive. It is up to you, the manager, to train, motivate and supervise the staff to ensure your success and to keep customers coming back and spreading the word about your establishment.

The host or hostess is the first member of the restaurant staff whom the customer meets as he or she enters the dining room. For this reason he or she should make a good first impression by both his or her appearance and manner. Other requirements for the prospective hostess are that he or she has good posture, be well groomed, and present a neat and attractive appearance.

The host or hostess should use good English, and speak in a well-modulated tone of voice. He or she must be able to will the respect both of the customers and of the servers. The host or hostess should be interested in the business and loyal to the management. This combination of characteristics is found more often in well-educated persons than in those who have had fewer educational and social advantages, which explains the reason restaurateurs usually require a good educational background for hostess positions.

✕ Fast Fact

A pleasant expression and a friendly smile are as valuable to the host or hostess as poise and manners. By his or her appearance, bearing, and conduct, the host or hostess must be able to gain the goodwill of both customers and employees.

The host or hostess represents the management in the minds of most of the customers, and he or she is also the teacher and leader of the employees who are under his or her supervision. He or she should, therefore, be honest, truthful, loyal and dependable. The conduct of the host or hostess, both when on duty and when outside of the restaurant, should be of a kind to command respect, and to elicit favorable comment both upon herself/himself and upon the establishment by which he or she is employed.

Following are a few rules that should govern the business relationships of the host or hostess:

In his or her relationship with the restaurant management, the host or hostess should show that he or she is:

- Loyal to the business and its policies.

- Able to follow regulations and carry out directions.

- Willing to assume responsibility.

- Has initiative in discovering and planning new and better methods of doing the work.

- Able to take criticism and to profit by it.

In his or her relationship with customers, the host or hostess should:

- Be pleasant in manner and show a willingness to be of service.

- Be courteous and tactful in an effort to prevent misunderstandings.

- Be impartial in rendering service and thus prevent charges of favoritism on the part of customers.

- Attempt to make reasonable adjustments of customer complaints.

- Be careful to uphold high standards of food service.

In his or her contacts with coworkers, the host or hostess should:

- Be friendly but should discourage over-familiarity.

- Show sincere interest in the restaurant's work and should cooperate with fellow workers in giving customers good service.

- Be impartial and fair in working with associates.

- Be good-tempered and serene, even under trying circumstances.

- Direct personnel and handle personnel difficulties with courage and firmness.

- Assume the attitude of the teacher who makes constructive criticism, avoids unnecessary faultfinding, and gives praise cheerfully when it is merited.

- Assume the attitude of the executive who respects the worth of the individual and who believes that "to lead" is better than "to drive."

Inspecting the Dining Room

The host or hostess is responsible for the appearance, cleanliness and order of the dining room during the serving period. Before the meal service begins, he or she should make a check to be sure that:

1. The main dining room, private rooms, booths and counters are clean and in good order. Any disorder should be reported to the proper authority and remedied before the meal service begins.

2. Window curtains, Venetian blinds and window roller-shades are adjusted to furnish satisfactory light.

3. The temperature and ventilation of the dining room are properly adjusted.

4. Tables are arranged properly and completely equipped.

5. Serving stands and side tables are properly arranged and have adequate supplies.

6. There are enough menu cards, and they are distributed properly.

7. Order forms and sharpened pencils are provided.

8. Table reservations and "reserved" signs have been placed.

9. The tables arranged for special parties are ready, and flowers, candles and other decorations provided.

10. Flowers are fresh and attractively arranged. Plants should be inspected for proper care, pruning and watering.

11. There is an adequate supply of tablecloths, table pads, doilies, napkins and serving towels.

12. Necessary repairs have been made to furnishings and fixtures.

Providing Excellent Service

Among the ways which the hostess may use to ensure good service are:

- See that orders are taken as soon as customers are ready to give them. When the regular server is unavoidably detained, take the order or direct another server to do so.

- Watch the service at the various tables in order to avoid unnecessary delays between courses.

- Notify the server that the customers are ready for service when he or she has been busy elsewhere.

- Keep customers supplied with water, butter, bread, hot coffee and clean ashtrays as they are needed by notifying the server or bus person.

- Provide service for children as promptly as possible. Serve un-iced water to young customers and supply them with the special menus, favors and children's dishes provided by the restaurant.

- Summon the server to take the order when the customer requests additional food or supplementary service.

- Approve special orders for foods not on the regular menu and requests for substitutions in the menu.

- Present the dessert menu to guests who have completed the main course and are waiting for further service.

- Conserve menus and keep them by collecting them from tables and side stands during the meal period.

- Be courteous and agreeable to all guests but do not engage in long conversations that appear to favor particular customers or that divert his or her attention from the service of other guests.

- If time permits, assist departing guests with their wraps and bid them "good-bye." Express the hope that the service was satisfactory and that they will come again.

- Have tables cleared and reset promptly after the guests leave them.

- Check supplies and linen at the close of the meal period to determine the amount on hand. See that they are given proper care and that they are put away properly.

Supervising the Service

The primary function of the food service host or hostess is to dispense hospitality as a representative of the management. When receiving customers, the host should greet them graciously and try to make them feel that they are welcome and will receive good service. A pleasant reception, careful service throughout the meal, and courteous treatment as they leave will impress customers with the excellence of the service, and it will make them feel that their patronage is appreciated.

✖ Fast Fact

The feeling of being a valued patron is what converts the occasional customer into a regular guest.

Food service is one of mankind's oldest forms of hospitality and is associated in one's mind with courtesy, cheerfulness and goodwill. The host should realize that goodwill toward the establishment is created by courteous and interested service, just as it is lost by unwilling and indifferent service.

The host has working relations with all the individuals concerned with sales and service: the manager, the waitstaff and the guests. He must interpret management's policies and standards to the customers; and he must convey the wishes of both the management and the guests to the sales staff. The skill with which he conducts himself in this pivotal position will determine to a considerable extent the efficiency of the service and the satisfaction of the guests.

The Nature of Host Work

The food service host represents the management to the customer; he conveys the wishes of both the management and the customer to the sales staff and kitchen force; he reports to the management recommendations, suggestions and complaints from both the customers and employees. Good judgment and tact on his part, therefore, are essential. When the restaurant is large and there are several dining rooms, more than one host will be necessary to receive guests and supervise service. In large food service operations, therefore, the host usually has assistant hosts, captains or head waitpersons who are responsible for supervising a section of the dining room or for the execution of specific duties involved in serving guests. It should be understood that the "duties of the host" discussed in this unit include all duties that may be executed by the host or by any of his or her assistants.

Performing Clerical Work

Some clerical duties are usually assigned to the host. The amount of these for which he is responsible depends upon the organization of the restaurant, the size of the supervisory staff and the number of office employees. From among the clerical duties, the host may:

- Check printed menus with the kitchen menu to discover omissions, inaccuracies or corrections, and change menus accordingly.

- Fill out storeroom requisitions for supplies such as matches, paper doilies, paper inserts for metal dishes, candles, nuts and condiments.

- Record reservations for tables and special parties; include all necessary information on a reservation form.

- Record the service hours of dining room employees on the daily time sheet (if a time clock is not used).

- Fill out the linen report.

- Fill out or assist with the sales analysis for the meal.

- Report to the manager, in writing, any important suggestions, serious complaints or compliments from customers.

Making Arrangements for Special Parties

Unless there is a supervisor in charge of catering, the host generally takes reservations for special parties. He may improve his ability to handle this business by following the regulations of the management—concerning maximum and minimum size for special groups, minimum charges, number of courses, food choices allowed at a given price, time and guarantee of number—and by obtaining the necessary information from the person making the reservation, including:

- Name, address and telephone number of the person calling.

- The name of the organization, if one is involved.

- Day, date and hour of reservation.

- Occasion.

- Probable number in the group, and number of guests guaranteed.

- Preferences as to table location and dining room (main or private).

- Price or price range.

- Whether sample menus are to be mailed.

- Arrangements for flowers and decorations.

- Arrangements for payment of the sales check (is the check to be paid in one amount or is the money to be collected individually?).

When a table reservation is made, obtain the following information:

1. Name of person making the reservation.

2. Number of persons included in the reservation.

3. Date and time.

4. Preference of table location.

5. Arrangements for flowers.

6. Whether a special menu is desired or guests will make their selections from the regular menu.

✕ Fast Fact

Customers who don't show up for their reservations can eat away at a restaurant's profits. To avoid this, get customers' phone numbers and make one or two follow-up calls to confirm their reservation.

Serving Special Parties

The general responsibilities of the host for the service of a special party include such duties as:

1. Securing and assigning the extra waitstaff and buspersons needed for service.

2. Rearranging the serving schedule to allow use of regular employees.

3. Making out the orders for liners and dishes.

4. Giving instructions for setting tables.

5. Checking set tables for completeness, arrangement and appearance.

6. Checking to be sure that the correct number of places has been set.

7. Giving the necessary general instructions to individual servers.

8. Giving specific instructions to individual servers.

9. Notifying the kitchen staff of the time when the service will be required.

10. Notifying the kitchen staff when they should begin serving each course.

11. Signaling the head waitperson when it is time to begin placing each course.

12. Signaling the head waitperson when it is time to begin removing the dishes from each course.

13. Approving and supplying special services that may be requested by customers, such as tea instead of coffee, fish instead of meat, bread instead of rolls, and foods for persons on special diets.

14. Providing supplies that may be requested, such as a pitcher of water for the speaker's place, a change tray for the person collecting the money at the table, change for the person selling tickets at the door, or an easel or blackboard for the speaker. Anticipate these requests in advance of the meal service, so far as possible, in order that the proper provision may be made. Otherwise, satisfy such requests to your best ability when they are made.

Receiving Customers

The host should receive customers in a gracious, yet dignified manner. He should endeavor to make the guests feel welcome and assured that they will receive satisfactory service. With this in mind, he may:

- Stand near the entrance to the dining room in order to greet customers as they arrive and seat them promptly. This responsibility is often assigned to an assistant host when the host is charged with supervisory or service duties.

- Greet the customers with a pleasant smile and nod, using the appropriate greeting—"Good morning," "Good afternoon," or "Good evening"—and greeting customers by name whenever possible.

- When a checkroom is located near the entrance, suggest that guests check hats, wraps, umbrellas and packages.

- Ask how many are in each group and seat the group at a suitable table. Avoid the use of a table for four to seat one or two persons unless no smaller tables are available.

- Ask the customers' preference with regard to table location when the dining room is not too crowded.

- Walk slightly ahead of the customers when escorting them to a table.

- Seat couples at small tables or in booths. Place disabled and elderly persons near the entrance so they will not be required to walk far. Seat men or women who come alone at small tables, but avoid placing them behind a post, near the entrance doorway or in the direct path to the kitchen doors.

- Ask permission before seating strangers together, doing so only when the dining room is so crowded that this procedure is unavoidable. First explain the probable length of time the guest will have to wait for a private table, then ask if he or she would mind sharing a table with someone else. Avoid seating a man with a woman who is dining alone, or taking a woman to a table where a man is already seated unless they are acquaintances and are willing to share a table.

- Apportion the seating of customers to the several serving stations so that no one section of the dining room will be overcrowded.

- When customers must wait for tables, seat them where they are available, or indicate a place to stand that is out of the way of traffic.

- Have the table cleared of soiled dishes and reset before customers are seated.

- Pull out the chair for a female guest and help her arrange her wraps and packages.

- Indicate a rack where a man may hang his hat and overcoat, if no checkroom is provided.

- Provide a junior chair for small children and a highchair for infants in arms. Offer to help seat the child and arrange the napkin or bib if the mother wishes this service.

- Place the opened menu before each guest, from the left side, or instruct the captain or waiter to do so.

- Fill the water glasses or instruct the busperson or waitperson to do so promptly.

Chapter 4
Table Service

If you asked the average American to describe a restaurant's table service, they would most likely paint the simple picture of customer sitting down at a table and having their food brought to them. Sure, most customers sit down and have their food brought to them. However, the way in which the food is brought to a customer is where we can start categorizing things. With the wide variety of restaurants in the world, it's only natural that there are different types of table service.

As mentioned, table service is the way in which a restaurant staff serves its customers' food. No one method is better than the other, and most of them can be used appropriately depending on the venue. Restaurant managers strive to give commendable service to their guests, and good food service is achieved by adopting a suitable method of service, training the sales force in it, and requiring each waitstaff member to follow the specified procedure. This policy results in a uniform standard of service that makes your restaurant unique and more efficient. Let's take a look at the different types of table service below.

American Service

American table service is "combination" service, which is a compromise among the two or more traditional forms of service that originated in other countries. If, for instance, the soup course is served in a tureen and dipped into the soup plates at the table in the "English" fashion, the main course served on dinner plates from the kitchen or serving pantry in the "Russian" manner, and the salad course offered from a large bowl and served by the waitperson in the "French" style, three forms of service are combined in a single meal. The traditional forms of table service most commonly used in catering to the public are named for the countries in which the services originated: France, Russia and England. Because these traditional methods have been adapted to American usage, it is interesting to consider briefly how they affect modern table service in the United States.

✗ Fast Fact

According to the National Restaurant Organization, 61 percent of consumers said they would order delivery from a table service restaurant if offered.

French Service

The most elaborate form of table service is the "French" service used in some exclusive clubs, hotels and restaurants. In the French service, the waitperson usually serves the guests from a food wagon or a side table. Attractive, tastefully arranged dishes of food are always presented to the guest for inspection before serving. The waiter then serves the individual plates from the platter, serving bowl or chafing dish, as the case may be.

In a modification of French service called "platter service," the food is arranged attractively on serving dishes supplied with silver and offered to the guest so that he may serve himself. A single dish or the entire main course may be served in this way. In some restaurants, serving dishes of fresh-cooked vegetables of a fine quality are thus offered to each guest for selection; others serve attractive compartment trays of assorted relishes. Trays of assorted small cakes are sometimes offered after frozen desserts have been placed. French pastries frequently are offered to customers on a tray.

Another variation of the French service is the salad cart now popular in some restaurants and tea rooms. Salads are placed on the cart and wheeled to tables so that the guests may make their selections. The waitperson arranges the individual servings at the cart and places them at each guest's cover. Another variation of French service is the custom practiced in some restaurants of having the waitperson bring to the guest trays of assorted individual salads or assorted desserts from which to make a selection.

English Service

The "English" style of service is sometimes called "host service." When this service is used, the platters and serving dishes are placed before the host or hostess, who serves the individual plates. The waiter stands at the right of the host, receives the served plate from him and places it before each guest. Female guests are sometimes served first, then men; however, the usual procedure is to serve each guest in turn, beginning with the person seated to the right of the server. Commercial food service units do not use English service for the main course of the meal except upon request in connection with private parties. A patron may ask for this type of service on some special occasion, such as a family dinner party or Thanksgiving Day, when, for instance, the host wishes to carve the turkey at the table and to serve the individual plates himself.

Occasionally the English style of service is used in serving the beverage course, perhaps at the tea hours. A tray containing the tea or after-dinner coffee service is placed before the hostess in order that the hostess may serve her guests.

Special desserts and forms of ice cream are sometimes served with host service. During the Christmas season a traditional "blazing plum pudding" may be brought to the table for guests to have the pleasure of watching the flames and seeing it served. A birthday cake may be set before the guest of honor, who is expected to "make a wish and blow out the candles" and cut the first slice or serve all of the guests. In each of these cases, a particularly attractive dish is served at the table as an expression of hospitality on the part of the host or hostess. Variations of English service are frequently used in noncommercial operations, such as college dining halls.

Russian Service

When the "Russian" form of service is followed, individual portions of food are placed on the plates in the kitchen or serving pantry, garnished and ready to serve. The Russian method is used by most restaurants for serving meals as well as banquets.

Buffet Service

Buffets are used by some establishments for serving appetizer and salad courses. Occasionally an entire meal is served in buffet fashion. For buffet service, a table is attractively set with a variety of foods; each guest is given a large service plate, sometimes chilled or heated, and walks along the table helping herself.

Under the usual procedure for restaurant buffet service, the waitperson serves breads, beverages and desserts at each table. When hot foods are included, a cook or server carves the roast, and helpers serve vegetables and other foods from casseroles, chafing dishes and bowls.

Family-Style

Family-style service is a modification of American service. For family-style service, preparation, including cutting foods and slicing meats, is done in the kitchen. The food is served in large bowls or on large platters and passed around the table by the guests. This service is closest to the way we eat in our own homes and the work of a server is very minimal in this type of venue. Servers generally set the table, get drinks, bring out the platters, remove dirty dishes and present the check.

Left or Right?

One main rule servers can follow is that women are generally waited on before the men. Use the following serving suggestions as a guide:

Appetizers and salads

Appetizers and salads should be served from the right with the right hand. The flatware for appetizers and salads is usually already on the table.

Soups

If soup is being served, make sure the bowl is on a plate. Add a nice touch, with a doily underneath the bowl. Soup spoons should be set to the right of the bowl and soup served from the right.

Entrée

Entrées are also served from the right, placed so the main element of the plate faces the guest. Flatware for the entrée should be placed on the table before the entrée arrives. Be sure the servers only touch the flatware by the handle and plates by the rim. If side dishes are served on separate plates, they should be served from the left.

Dessert

When serving dessert, the waitperson should place the utensil to the guest's left and serve the dessert from the right.

Beverages

Drinks are served from the right and coffee is poured from the right.

Clearing

In general, all plates and other dishes should be cleared from the right.

Signs that a guest is done

These signals include placing a napkin on top of the plate, pushing the plate to the side and turning the fork upside down across the plate, or both knife and fork placed together at an angle on the plate. However, even if your server sees these signals at a table, he or she should first ask the guests before they clear.

Resources

For more information on serving etiquette, visit WebstaurantStore's website at **www.webstaurantstore.com/article/90/fine-dining-etiquette-for -servers.html**. For wine-serving etiquette, visit Tasting Wine at **www .tasting-wine.com/serving-wine-2/wine-etiquette**.

Table Side Service

Table side service is most often associated with fine dining restaurants, but it can be used in other venues as well. It is a good sales technique because it allows guests to view the preparation or display of various menu items. When preparing food table side, you need to be sure the food is fresh and attractive. Items should also be easy and quick to prepare and they should not produce offensive odors or smoke when cooked.

✖ Fast Fact

Be sure that everything is clean when preparing and serving a customer's food. You should not touch any of the food with your hands.

Some of the items that can be displayed or prepared table side include:

- Appetizers
- Salads
- Meats/Fish
- Desserts
- Bakery items
- Fruits

When preparing meats table side, be sure all fat and sinews have been removed from the meat product and cut the portions into a size that will cook in one minute.

Some of the preparation techniques that can be used table side include:

- Tossing
- Flambé
- Cooking
- Boning
- Carving

Tossing

When tossing salads table side, make sure greens are clean and thoroughly drained before putting them on the cart. Also be sure that all items are kept refrigerated until use. You can make the salad dressing in the kitchen or at the table.

Flambé

Flambé work involves lighting liquor in a pan. This technique is used for desserts such as Banana Foster and Crêpes Suzette. After lighting the cooking lamp, pour the proper quantity of liquor in a pan; cover the flame with the pan completely. Place the bottle of liquor far from the flame and allow the amount in the pan to warm. Move the pan off the center of the burner towards you and tilt the pan away from you just until the liquor comes in contact with the flame and ignites. As soon as the liquor ignites, lift the pan up slightly and slowly move it in a circular pattern so the flames move around the pan.

✖ *Fast Fact*

Caution must be used when cooking or flambéing table side. Make sure to periodically check burners and gas containers to be sure they are functioning properly. You should also be sure a hand-held fire extinguisher is easily accessible and keep the cart (or guéridon) at a safe distance from guests' tables.

Cooking

When deciding what to prepare table side, you need to take several things into consideration: the medium (clarified butter, oil, steaming, etc.), the length of time an item will take to cook, and the ability to create the appropriate flavors in the short cooking time you have when preparing foods table side. While one would never prepare a roast or sautéed chicken breast table side, you could consider sautéing vegetables or preparing a stir fry.

Boning

Some fine-dining establishments that serve whole fish will bone the cooked fish for patrons on a table side cart. This does require some special skills, so you would want to practice these skills before trying it in front of an audience.

To bone a fish:

1. Remove the head and tail.

2. With a fish knife, remove the skin carefully.

3. Remove the two upper fillets, starting at the head and letting your knife glide down between the bones and meat.

4. Turn the fish over and remove the other two fillets.

5. Arrange the fillets on a platter.

Carving

Carving can also be done tableside when serving an item such as a whole chicken. Again, this does require some special skills, so you would want to practice these skills before trying it in front of an audience. To carve table side, you will need a cutting board with a groove to catch juices, a slicer (this knife is ideal to cut long line slices from items such as smoked salmon), a pointed knife with a straight edge (this knife is used to carve poultry, a leg of lamb chateaubriand, etc.), a fork to help transfer the meat to the serving platter, and a warming platter.

To carve a whole chicken:

1. Lay the chicken on the cutting board sideways.

2. Hold the drumstick with a fork and using a short, strong knife, cut through the skin beneath the leg and remove the leg with the fork.

3. Remove the second leg in the same manner.

4. Remove both wings in the same manner.

5. Lay the chicken on its back and hold it steady with the fork.

6. With the knife tip, loosen the breast meat from the bone.

7. Hold the carcass with the knife and remove the breast meat with the fork.

8. Arrange the chicken pieces on a platter.

To carve boneless meat (such as tenderloin):

1. Place the meat on the cutting board.

2. With the back of a fork, press on the meat slightly to hold in place (do not pierce the meat with the fork or all the juices will run out).

3. Slice the meat on a bias.

4. Place the pieces on a platter.

Table Settings

All of your front-of-the-house staff should be trained on correct table settings. Generally, each member of the waitstaff is assigned to a group of tables. These sections are known as "stations." A waitperson may keep a reserve supply of silver, glasses, china and linen at a side table and serve from it. Reserve supplies of condiments, ice, water and butter are often kept on the table also, as well as a thermos of hot coffee. There is space for the serving tray either on the serving table or on a separate tray rack.

The waitperson should provide tables that are properly set before service is given—with clean linen, polished silver, shining glassware and spotless china. Tables should be promptly cleared after service and reset as needed. When a side table is used, the waitperson is responsible for including a supply of extra serving equipment and the required foods and stock supplies, arranged in an orderly manner on a clean surface.

He or she should provide tables that are:

- Properly set before service is given.

- Carefully arranged with clean linen, polished silver, shining glassware and spotless china.

- Promptly cleared after service.

- Reset as they are needed.

Setting the Table

The cover

This is the space—about 24 inches by 15 inches—within which one place is set with china, silver, linen and glass. An imaginary line may be drawn defining this area to assist in laying the cover.

Linen

A silence pad, if used, should be placed evenly on the table so that the edges do not hang down below the tablecloth. The tablecloth is laid over the silence pad or undercover or directly over the table, with the center fold up and equidistant from the edges of the table. All four corners should fall an even distance from the floor. The cloth should be free from wrinkles, holes and stains.

When doily service is used, the doilies should be laid in the center of the cover, about 1 inch from the edge of the table. Silverware is placed on the doily.

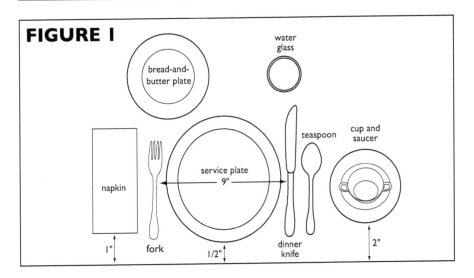

FIGURE 1. "Table Cover Setup" using 16" x 12" doily and showing space allowance for a 24" cover arrangement.

1. Napkin

2. Fork

3. Bread-and-butter plate

4. Service plate

5. Water glass

6. Dinner knife

7. Teaspoon

8. Cup and saucer

The folded napkin is placed at the left of the fork, with open corners at the lower right and about 1 inch from the front edge of the table.

✗ Fast Fact

For formal dinners when a service plate is used, napkins may be folded and placed on the service plate.

Silver

Knives and forks should be laid about 9 inches apart, so that a dinner plate may be easily placed between them. The balance of the silverware is then placed to the right of the knife and to the left of the fork in the order in which it is to be used (placing the first-used at the outside and proceeding toward the plate). The handles of all silver should be perpendicular to the table edge and about 1 inch from the edge. Forks are placed at the left side of the cover, tines pointed up. Knives are placed at the right side of the cover with the cutting edge turned toward the plate.

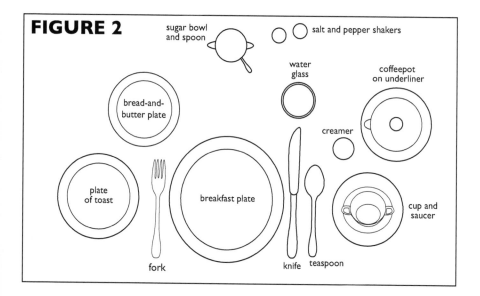

FIGURE 2. Cover arrangement for main breakfast course.

1. Plate of toast

2. Fork

3. Breakfast plate

4. Knife

5. Teaspoon

6. Saucer

7. Cup

8. Bread-and-butter plate

9. Water glass

10. Creamer

11. Coffeepot on underliner

12. Sugar bowl

13. Sugar spoon

14. Salt and pepper shakers

Spoons are laid, bowls up, at the right of the knives. The butter spreader is placed across the top edge or on the right side of the bread and butter plate, with the handle either perpendicular or parallel to the edge of the table, the cutting edge turned toward the butter plate. The butter spreader is properly used only when butter is served and a bread-and-butter plate is provided. Sometimes when a sharp steel-bladed knife is used for the meat course, a small, straight knife for butter is laid at the right of the meat knife.

Oyster and cocktail forks are placed at the extreme right of the cover beyond the teaspoons or laid across the right side of the service plate underlying the cocktail glass or the oyster service.

Silver for dessert service—the iced teaspoon and the parfait, or sundae, spoon—are placed just before the respective course at the right side of the cover. The dessert fork is laid at the right side of the cover if it is placed just before the dessert is served.

Breakfast or luncheon forks, salad forks and dessert forks are placed next to the plate in order of use; the spoons are arranged to the right of the forks, in order of use, beginning in each instance with the first course (on the outside) and working toward the center of the cover. When knives are not used in the cover, both the forks and spoons are placed to the right of the cover.

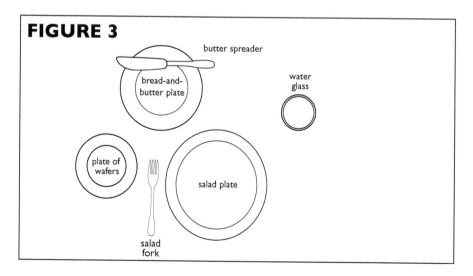

FIGURE 3. Cover arrangement when a dinner salad is served as separate course.

1. Plate of wafers

2. Salad fork

3. Salad plate

4. Bread-and-butter plate

5. Butter spreader

6. Water glass

China and glassware.

The bread-and-butter plate is placed at the left of the cover, directly above the tines of the meat fork. The water glass is placed at the right of the cover, immediately above the point of the dinner knife.

Wine, liquor and beer glasses, if applicable, are placed to the right of the water glass. When a butter chip is used, it is placed to the left and on a line with the water glass, toward the center or left side of the cover.

Sugar bowls and salt and pepper shakers are generally placed in the center of small tables. When wall tables for two are set, the sugar bowl and shakers usually are placed on the side nearest the wall or the side nearest the room rather than in the center of the table. When an open-topped sugar bowl is used, a clean sugar spoon is laid to the right of the bowl.

When a large table is being set up and several sets of sugars and creamers are needed, the cream pitchers and sugar bowls may be placed at equal distances down the center of the table. Guests can more conveniently handle them if the handles are turned toward the cover. When several sets of salt and pepper shakers are used on a large table, they may be placed between the covers on a line parallel with the bases of the water glasses.

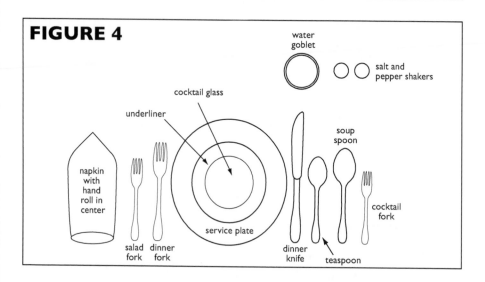

FIGURE 4. Cover arrangement for appetizer course of a formal dinner.

1. Napkin with hand roll in center

2. Salad fork

3. Dinner fork

4. Service plate

5. Underliner

6. Cocktail glass

7. Dinner knife

8. Teaspoon

9. Soupspoon

10. Cocktail fork

11. Water goblet

12. Salt and pepper shakers

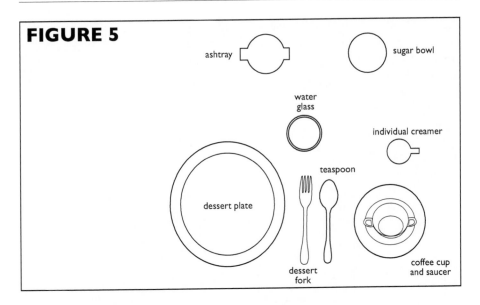

FIGURE 5. Cover arrangement for dessert course for luncheon or dinner.

1. Dessert plate

2. Dessert fork

3. Teaspoon

4. Coffee cup and saucer

5. Water glass

6. Individual creamer

7. Ashtray

8. Sugar bowl

Napkins should be folded carefully according to the style of the restaurant, with folds straight and edges even.

Menus always must be replaced with new ones if they become soiled or torn.

Flowers should be arranged in containers appropriate in color, size and shape.

Individual creamers should be washed and thoroughly cooled before being filled with cream. A container with a slender spout is used for filling if a cream dispenser is not available. Care should be taken not to fill creamers too full.

Ashtrays should be collected and cleaned frequently, especially during the serving period; a clean one should be provided each time newly arrived guests are seated at the table.

Serving trays should be kept clean and dry to protect both the waitperson's uniform and the serving-table surface. The top of the tray should be wiped clean before it is loaded to prevent the bottoms of the dishes from being soiled.

Ice cubes or cracked ice should be clean and free of foreign matter; ice cubes should be handled with tongs and cracked ice with a special scoop or serving spoon. Ice should be transported in containers dedicated for ice only. Ice should be considered a food item.

Butter pots need to be chilled and a pan of ice made ready before serving.

Chairs should have crumbs dusted off after each guest has left. Backs, rounds and legs of chairs should be carefully dusted every day.

Silver or stainless should be cleaned according to the special directions of the restaurant. When a cream polish is used, it should be rubbed with a soft cloth or a small brush over the surface and well into the embossed pattern of the silverware. The silver should then be thoroughly washed, rinsed and polished with a dry cloth to remove all traces of the silver cream.

General Rules for Table Service

Since there are several methods of table service, each food service unit must follow the method appropriate to its particular conditions, and each member of the waitstaff must learn to follow the serving directions exactly so that service will be uniform throughout the unit. The following rules are approved by social custom:

- Place and remove all food from the left side of the guest.

- Place and remove all beverages, including water, from the right of the guest.

- Use the left hand to place and remove dishes when working at the left side of the guest, and the right hand when working at the right side of the guest. This provides free arm action for the server and avoids the danger of bumping against the guest's arm.

- Place each dish on the table, the four fingers of your left hand under the lower edge and your thumb on the upper edge of the plate.

- Never reach in front of the guest, nor across one person in order to serve another.

- Present serving dishes from the left side, in a position so that the guest can serve himself. Place serving silver on the right side of the dish, with the handles turned toward the guest so that he or she may reach and handle them easily.

- Do not place soiled, chipped or cracked glassware and china or bent or tarnished silverware before a guest.

- Hold silverware by the handles when it is laid in place. Be sure it is clean and spotless.

- Handle tumblers by their bases and goblets by their stems.

- Do not lift water glasses from the table to fill or refill; when they cannot be reached conveniently, draw them to a more convenient position.

- Set fruit juice and cocktail glasses, cereal dishes, soup bowls and dessert dishes on small plates before placing them in the center of the cover, between the knife and the fork.

- When it accompanies the main course, place the salad plate at the left of the forks, about 2 inches from the edge of the table. When the salad is served as a separate course, place it directly in front of the guest.

- Place individual serving trays or bread and rolls above and to the left of the forks. Place a tray or basket of bread for the use of several guests toward the center of the table.

- Place the cup and saucer at the right of the spoons, about 2 inches from the edge of the table. Turn the handle of the cup to the right, either parallel to the edge of the table or at a slight angle toward the guest.

- Set tea and coffee pots on small plates and place above and slightly to the right of the beverage cup. Set iced beverage glasses on coasters or small plates to protect tabletops and linen.

- Place individual creamers, syrup pitchers and small lemon plates above and a little to the right of the cup and saucer.

- Place a milk glass at the right of and below the water glass.

- Serve butter, cheese and cut lemon with a fork. Serve relishes, pickles and olives with a fork or spoon, not with the fingers.

More and more, food service operations are using booth- or banquet-type seating. It is extremely difficult to carry out proper table service in these situations. The general rules for booth service are:

Serve everything with the hand farthest from the guest; use your right hand to serve a guest at your left and your left hand to serve a guest to your right.

Remove soiled plates with the hand nearest your guest while substituting the next course with the hand farthest from your guest.

Breakfast service

Good breakfast service is important because many customers are in a hurry, some have little appetite, and others are "out of sorts" until they have had their coffee. A cheerful attitude on the part of the waitstaff and prompt and efficient service, therefore, may help customers "start the day right."

Foods served for breakfast are most palatable when they are freshly prepared and when they are served at the correct temperature. The waitperson, therefore, should serve breakfast in courses unless the customer especially requests that the whole order be served at once. Cooked foods and hot beverages should be brought to the customer directly from the serving station and under no circumstances allowed to remain on the serving stand to cool while the customer finishes a preceding course.

 **Fast Fact**

When asked, seven out of 10 consumers said they wished that restaurants would serve breakfast all day long.[3]

Order of breakfast service

1. When fresh fruit or fruit juice is ordered, it is desirable to serve it first, and then to remove the soiled dishes before placing the toast and coffee.

2. When customers order a combination of cooked fruit, toast and coffee, they may ask to have the whole order served at once. Place the fruit dish, set on an underliner, in the center of the cover, the plate of toast at the left of the forks and the coffee at the right of the teaspoons.

3. The National Restaurant Organization, 2016

3. When the breakfast order includes a cereal and a hot dish, the service procedure may be as follows:

   a. Place the fruit course in the center of the cover.

   b. Remove the fruit service.

   c. Place the cereal bowl, set on an underliner, in the center of the cover. Cut individual boxes of cereal partway through the side near the top so the guest may open them easily.

   d. Remove the cereal service.

   e. Place the breakfast plate of eggs, meat or other hot food in the center of the cover. Place the plate of toast at the left of the forks. Place the coffee service at the right of the spoons.

   f. Remove the breakfast plate and the bread plate.

   g. Place the finger bowl, filled one-third full of warm water. At times the finger bowl is placed after the fruit course when fruits that may soil the fingers have been served.

   h. Place the sales check, face down, at the right of the cover or present it on a clean change tray.

Luncheon service

Luncheon customers usually can be classified in two groups: Businesspeople who have a short lunch period and want quick service, and shoppers and hostess groups who want more leisurely service. The duty of the waiter/waitress is to avoid keeping customers in the first group waiting for service, and to avoid making those in the second group feel they are being rushed.

Order of service for luncheon

1. Fill the water glasses three-fourths full of iced water.

2. Place chilled butter on a cold bread-and-butter plate.

3. Place the appetizer in the center of the cover.

4. Remove the appetizer when the guest has finished.

5. Place the soup service in the center of the cover.

6. Remove the soup service.

7. Place the entrée plate in center of cover.

8. Place individual vegetable dishes (if used) above the cover.

9. If salad is served with the main course, place the salad at the left of the forks, about 2 inches from edge of table.

10. Place tray or basket of bread and rolls at the left of the salad plate.

11. Place hot beverages above and a little to the right of the cup and saucer, with individual creamer above the cup.

12. Place an iced beverage or milk at the right and a little below the water glass.

13. Remove the main-course dishes.

14. Remove any extra silver not used for the main course.

15. Crumb the table, if necessary.

16. Place desert silver to the right of the cover, with fork nearest the dessert plate, if fork and teaspoon are used. When several teaspoons are placed, the dessert fork may be laid on the left side, to "balance the cover."

17. Place the dessert service in center of the cover.

18. Serve hot coffee if requested.

19. Remove dessert dishes and silver.

20. Place the fingerbowl on the underliner (when one is used) in the center of the cover.

21. Present the check, face down.

Dinner service

Because dinner guests are seldom in a hurry, their waitperson is able to give them a more leisurely type of service than is possible at breakfast or lunch.

Although the guest should be allowed plenty of time to complete each course, long waits between courses should be avoided. The waitperson should observe the guests during the meal in order to serve the next course promptly and to comply with any requests made by the guests for special service.

Order of dinner service

1. From the left, place the appetizer or hors d'oeuvres service in the center of the cover. A tray of canapés and hors d'oeuvres is often offered to the guest. In this case, an empty plate should first be placed before the guest and the tray of hors d'oeuvres then offered.

2. Remove the first-course dishes.

3. Place the soup service in the center of the cover.

4. Remove the soup service.

5. When the entrée is served on a platter, place it directly above the cover. Lay the serving silver at the right of the platter. Place the warm dinner plate in the center of the cover.

6. When plate, or "Russian," service is used, place the dinner plate in the center of the cover.

7. Place salad at the left of the forks when it is served with the main course.

8. Place beverages to the right of teaspoons.

9. Offer rolls or place them to the left of the salad plate.

10. Remove the main-course dishes when the guest has finished.

11. When salad is served as a separate course following the main course, place the salad fork at the left and the salad plate in the center of the cover.

12. Remove the salad service.

13. Crumb the table if necessary.

14. Place silver for the dessert course.

15. Place the dessert service in the center of the cover.

16. Serve hot coffee or place the demitasse.

Special attentions to observe when serving:

1. Serve hot food hot and on heated dishes.

2. Serve cold food chilled and on cold dishes.

3. Inquire how food is to be cooked:

    a. Eggs: fried or boiled; how many minutes.

    b. Steak: rare, medium-rare, medium, medium-well, or well-done.

    c. Toast: buttered or dry.

4. Refill water glasses whenever necessary during the meal.

5. Serve extra butter when needed.

6. Refill coffee on request and according to management policies. Bring more cream if necessary.

7. Serve granulated sugar with fresh fruit and unsweetened iced drinks.

8. Place silver necessary for a course just prior to serving.

    a. Soup spoons on extreme right of teaspoons.

    b. Cocktail fork to right of soupspoon.

9. Offer crackers, melba toast, and other accompaniments or relishes with appetizer and soup courses, according to policies of management.

10. Provide iced teaspoons for ice drinks and place parfait spoons when a parfait is served. Place soda spoons and straws with malted milks, milkshakes and ice cream sodas.

Setting an Elegant Table

One of a server's first duties is to check his or her tables before service begins to be sure everything is set up properly.

Here are the general steps in setting up tables:

- Rinse tables with sanitizing solution and a damp cloth before setting.

- Check seats for any crumbs or stickiness.

- Make sure tablecloths are the correct size. Place the center fold on the center of the table and open it to cover the table.

- Set up covers (china, silverware, napkins and glassware). Make sure to handle glassware by stems and plates by edges, making sure nothing is chipped, cracked or dirty.

- Make sure centerpieces are clean and fresh if they include flowers or candles.

- Fold napkins and place at settings.

Folding Napkins

The fold of napkins in an establishment is important in setting the ambiance. Usually more casual establishments will use simpler folds, and fine-dining venues will use more elaborate folding techniques. Make sure you begin with clean, ironed napkins. Napkins come in different sizes: dinner napkins are 18–24 inches; cocktail napkins are usually 4–6 inches. There are many different types of napkin folds and any of these would make your tables more festive and elegant. Here is a list of some of the most popular napkins folds:

- Iris fold

- Danish candle fold

- Dinner fold

- Cascade fold

- Kite envelope fold

- Bat fold

- Flirt fold

You can also add items to napkins, such as napkin rings. Other ideas include using fresh flowers, fresh herbs or nametags. To include a fresh flower with your napkins, you will need twine, a napkin, a strand of vine such as ivy and a fresh flower. Lay a cloth napkin out on the table. Pick it up by the center point, then lay the folded napkin back on the table and tie it with twine about 3 inches down from the point. Next, take the strand of vine and coil it, then lay it on the twine. Add the blossom to the center of the ivy coil.

To use a fresh herb with your napkin display you will need fresh herbs, a napkin and a piece of thin cord or twine. Fold a cloth napkin into a square and place it on the table at a diagonal. Tuck the points on left and right sides under the napkin. Cluster several sprigs of fresh herbs together and tie them with a thin cord in a loose knot. Place the herbs in the center of the napkin.

If you are setting up for a buffet or a special party such as a wedding rehearsal dinner, you may want to include nametags as part of your napkin presentation. Fold the napkin as you did for the fresh flower display—lay the napkin out, then pick it up by the very center point and let the sides drape down. Using a piece of cut ribbon and a fabric pen, write the guests' names on ribbon and snip a V shape out of the ends. Wrap a ribbon around each folded napkin.

Centerpieces

Centerpieces also should reflect the ambiance of the dining room. They may also reflect the time of year or a specific theme. They should be below eye level or on a stand above eye level so guests can see each other across the table. A centerpiece can be made from many things: fresh flowers, candles, mirrors, wood, copper pipes, etc.

Here are some simple centerpiece ideas:

- Dried flowers

- Fresh flowers in vases

- Silk flowers

- Chianti bottles with candles

- Candles

- Potted plants

- Pumpkin or other squash with fresh or dried flowers

- Container of seashells

- Hurricane lamps

- Glass vases filled with colored glass stones

Whatever type of centerpiece is used, servers must be given instructions on how to maintain the centerpieces. If using fresh flowers, servers should be instructed to change the flowers whenever they start to look wilted. Silk and dried flowers will need to be kept free of dust, as will candles and any other object used in the centerpiece, such as a basket or vase. Candles should also be replaced frequently so they look clean and fresh.

Chapter 5
Taking Orders

If you've been in the restaurant business for a while, taking orders may seem like second nature to you. Without batting an eye, you can jump in front of a collection of strangers, get a feel for the table, take their orders, and have an answer for every question they throw at you. However, new employees generally aren't prepared to tackle this challenge—even if they're fresh from working at another establishment. Don't allow a new employee to wait a table without making sure he or she knows the basics of taking an order and is familiar with your menu. This information can easily be taught with role playing exercises or by shadowing. Before the new servers are let loose on the floor, you may want to consider having them wait on you as a sort of "final exam." This way, you'll be certain they're taking orders properly.

Here are some useful guidelines to give your employees. The following information will help you organize your presentation for this training topic.

Customers usually like to have time to study the menu without feeling that their waiter is waiting impatiently to take the order. The waiter should be ready to give prompt attention as soon as the guest has decided on her order. The waiter stands at the left of the customer, close enough to hear her easily and to answer her questions distinctly. If the customer makes out a written order, the waiter should read it back to her and ask for any special instructions that may apply. When the waiter writes the order, his writing should be legible, the abbreviations correct, and the number of guests and table number indicated.

When a group of people is being served, the waiter should try to discover whether there is a host or hostesses for the group to whom he may go for instructions. While taking the order, he should ask for all the information he needs to serve the meal satisfactorily. For example:

- The food choices for each course.

- How the eggs, for instance, are to be cooked.

- Whether toast is to be dry or buttered.

- Whether meat is preferred rare, medium or well-done.

- Whether a sandwich is to be served plain or toasted.

- What kind of dressing is preferred for the salad.

- Whether coffee is to be served with the main course or with the dessert.

- Whether coffee is preferred hot or iced.

- Whether black or green tea is desired.

- Whether lemon or cream is preferred with tea.

Printed order forms, usually called "checks," are available in book form, numbered consecutively. When issued a book of checks, each member of the waitstaff is responsible for the numbers he or she receives. Spoiled checks therefore must not be destroyed; corrections should be made by drawing a line through the incorrect item—never by erasing it. The manager should approve these corrections. The check is issued as a means of recording the order, as the customer's bill, and as a source of information about the sale. Duplicate checks are used in filling orders in the kitchen.

✗ Fast Fact

A server's handwriting should be easy to read. A poorly written order can slow down the kitchen staff or, even worse, botch the customer's food.

Giving and Collecting Orders

The procedures used for giving and collecting orders in the kitchen vary somewhat with the organization, layout and regulations of the restaurant. However, certain general methods are applicable anywhere and help to determine the speed of the service as well as the condition and appearance of the food when it is placed before the customer. When the waiter is courteous and considerate in giving and assembling his order, he helps to maintain harmonious relations between the kitchen and dining room personnel.

The layout of the kitchen and the number of service stations will determine the routing the waitperson must follow in assembling an order. One new to the establishment must learn as quickly as possible the functions of each unit and exactly what foods and supplies are available at each station.

The waiter gives an order by placing a written order on a spindle provided for the purpose, or by giving the order to the expediter to "call." Orders may also be sent to the kitchen from a point-of-sale system or "Wireless

Waiter," as described below. When a written order is used, the waitperson uses his or her initials or number to identify it.

The waitstaff should not make a habit of saying they are in a hurry for their orders; the cooks are probably doing their best to fill orders quickly and in rotation. When extra-fast service is really necessary, a waitperson may be justified in asking to be served rapidly or even out of turn.

Timing the order

The waitperson should know when he or she will need a course and the amount of time the meal will take to prepare in the kitchen, especially when foods are cooked to order.

Assembling the order

Food requiring the longest time to prepare should be ordered first. The waitperson should plan the assembling of the order so that she can pick up each item as soon as possible after it has been dished. This will ensure food is served when it is at the correct temperature and will prevent it from crowding the serving counters. The following general sequence is recommended:

1. When the order is being filled, collect all the needed serving equipment and cold accompaniments such as bread, crackers, relishes, butter and cream.

2. Pick up cold foods next, taking care to keep them away from hot food on the tray.

3. The hot food should be picked up last. Cover soup to retain the heat. Cover the dinner plate with a hot cover when one is available.

4. If hot breads are served, pick them up last to serve them in their best condition.

5. When bowl or platter service is used, provide heated plates for hot foods and chilled plates for salads and other cold foods.

6. Rinse tea and coffee pots with hot water before filling them with hot beverages. Never pour iced drinks into warm glasses or place butter on a warm plate.

✂ Fast Fact

The appearance and temperature of food that is perfectly prepared in the kitchen can be spoiled in the service by a waitperson that is thoughtless, slow, or careless.

Approaching the Table

The server should approach a table within the first minute of customers being seating. This is the first impression your servers will make on your guests. Make sure they look professional and neat. Shirts should be tucked in and ironed, and aprons should be clean. The server should smile, make eye contact and greet the customers, giving the customers his or her name.

The server, a busser or the host should also bring water to the table during or before this exchange.

Giving a Friendly Greeting

Efficient service alone will not win the customer's goodwill or make the person want to return. Every effort should be made to make the customer feel that his or her patronage is appreciated and that everything possible will be done to satisfy the customer's wants. To accomplish this, the server should greet the customer in a friendly, courteous manner and be interested and attentive when taking and serving the order.

Although a friendly attitude is important in relations with the customer, the server's manner should be dignified and not too familiar. He or she should be businesslike in manner and not indulge in unnecessary conversation nor encourage banter. Under no circumstances should personal matters be discussed with a customer. The server's responsibility is to sell and to serve, not to entertain.

Giving Prompt Attention

Promptness in taking care of the customer is as important as greeting him in a friendly way. The hostess should watch for the entrance of guests into the dining room, the salesperson should closely observe her serving station and know when newly arrived guests are seated, and the counter server should be aware of the approach of customers wanting to be served.

The customer likes to be noticed, to be given a friendly greeting and desirable seating. He has come to the restaurant for good food and service and expects his wants to be satisfied.

Any special services, which the restaurant provides, that may be useful to the customer should be explained to him or her as the occasion arises. A few examples include:

1. A customer may want rapid service just before leaving on an early morning flight. When the restaurant has counter as well as table service, the customer should be told that he or she can be served more quickly if he or she will be seated at the counter.

2. A mother may ask for an extra plate so that she may share her lunch with her child. When children's service is available with a special food selection, smaller portions and lower prices, this service should be explained to her.

3. If a customer praises the hot homemade rolls, and the restaurant makes these available for takeout orders, offer this service to the customer.

4. When a customer comments on the attractiveness of the courtyard, he or she may be told that dinners are served there under the trees during the summer months.

Taking a Drink Order

When the server approaches the table for the first time, he or she should ask if anyone would like a drink. The server may want to make a suggestion or simply provide the customers with some information on what types of soft drinks or beers the restaurant carries. Be sure your servers know their drink jargon for this exchange; the guest that orders a vodka martini up with a twist will be miffed if he or she receives a gin martini on the rocks! This is also a good time to tell the table about any specials.

Serving the Drinks

Drinks should be served quickly. Make sure your servers put cocktail napkins under drink glasses. At this point, the server can ask if they are ready to order. If the table isn't ready, the server should check back with them within a reasonable amount of time. Tell your servers to look for clues that the table is ready. The most obvious clue is that everyone has closed the menus.

Explaining the Menu

The server should be thoroughly familiar with the menu contents, its arrangement and its prices. To illustrate:

1. Frequently a new customer is confused as to where to find certain items on the unfamiliar menu. The server should be quick to sense this uncertainty and to offer requested assistance in finding the desired articles.

2. Sometimes the customer fails to notice specials or some other featured group of foods on the menu. The server may tactfully indicate these to him.

3. A foreign name or an unfamiliar term on the menu may be perplexing to the reader. In response to her inquiry, a simple explanation of the meaning of the term or a description of the contents of the dish will be appreciated. The server should give such explanations graciously with an attitude of helpfulness, and never patronizingly or curtly.

4. A customer with poor eyesight may have difficulty in reading the menu. The server could read the items to him and write his order.

Taking the Food Order

Normal etiquette dictates that you start with the women at the table. If there are children, it is also appropriate to start with them. Again, take clues from the table. If one woman is obviously undecided, you may make her uncomfortable by insisting she places her order first. Let the others order, then come back to her. Make sure your servers have a thorough knowledge of the menu and can answer any questions about menu item preparation. If the customer asks or seems unsure, servers may also make recommendations at this point.

Delivering the Food

Make sure your servers know that food is served from the right side of the guest and plates are cleared from the right. Also, be sure that when your servers hold plates that they are only touching them on the edge. It's quite unappealing to see your server's thumb in your mashed potatoes!

Fast Fact

Servers should bring everyone's food at the same time. Make sure that they caution guests when plates are hot.

Checking Back

Be sure servers check back with guests within the first two to three minutes of being served. If there is a problem, the server will be able to take care of it immediately. Don't let the customer sit stewing and growing madder about a mistake.

Dessert

When the server is clearing the entrée plates or not long after, he or she should ask if the table wants desserts, coffees or after dinner drinks. You may want to supply servers with dessert menus or a dessert tray to show the customers. Servers could also make suggestions for desserts to split if everyone is feeling quite full. Often a table will split a dessert, and one sale is better than none!

Presenting the Check

The guest should not be kept waiting for her sales check. It should be presented either immediately after the last course has been served or as soon as she has finished eating. The check should be accurately totaled and laid face down on the table, to the right of the cover, on a small change tray. When a group of several persons has been served, the check should be placed by the host's cover; if the host is not known and the order has been written on one check, the check should be placed toward the center of the table. When a man and woman are dining together, the check should generally be presented near to the man, unless separate orders have been written. This is a judgment call, however; if in doubt, place the check in the middle of the table.

It is a courteous practice to ask if any other service is desired before present-ing the sales check and to thank the customer as the check is laid on the table. When a bill is received in payment, the waitperson should mention the denomination of the bill. When a credit card is presented, be sure to include a pen and the appropriate instruction, such as, "The top white copy is your copy and the bottom yellow copy is for the establishment." When tipping is sanctioned, the waitperson should leave the appropriate change. This will enable the customer to leave a gratuity, should she wish to do so.

Change should be placed on a change tray or tip tray provided for that purpose, not on a china plate, as coins make unnecessary noise when handled on china. Also, once the money is removed, the plate will appear clean, and it might later be used for food without being washed. It is incorrect for the waitperson to indicate in any way that a tip is expected or that any certain amount is anticipated. It is also discourteous to show disappointment because the tip was less than is customarily received. When a guest leaves a gratuity, she indicates her desire to reward the waitperson for services rendered.

When it looks obvious that the table is getting ready to go or when the customer asks for the check, the server should bring it, promptly. It's also a good idea for the server to explain the restaurant's payment procedures. He or she could say, "When you're ready, I'll come back to take care of that for you."

 **Fast Fact**

It's a nice touch for the server to say good-bye as the party is leaving. It leaves the customer with a friendly feeling. After all, they've just spent an hour or so in the company of your server!

Guests should be shown small courtesies when departing. For example, a waiter might draw out a woman's chair and assist with her wraps and packages. The waitperson should endeavor to say good-bye to all customers and to express the hope that they have enjoyed the meal or that they will come again. This sort of courtesy makes customers feel that they have been truly welcomed guests.

Clearing the Table

The following are standard procedures for clearing the table:

1. After any course, dishes should be removed from the left side, except the beverage service which should be removed from the right.

2. Platters and other serving dishes should be removed first when clearing the table, or they may be removed as soon as empty.

3. The main-course plate should be removed first, the salad plate next, followed by the bread-and-butter plate.

4. The empty milk or beverage glass is removed from the right side after the main course.

5. The table should be crumbed by using a small plate and a clean, folded napkin. This is especially important when hard rolls or crusty breads are served.

6. Hot tea and coffee service should be left on the table until the completion of the dessert course.

7. The water glass should remain on the table and be kept refilled as long as the guest is seated.

8. Replace soiled ashtrays with clean ones as often as necessary throughout the meal.

When a guest is seated at a table and it is necessary to change a soiled tablecloth, turn the soiled cloth halfway back, lay the clean cloth half open in front of the guest, and transfer the tableware to the clean cloth. The soiled cloth may then be drawn from the table and the clean one pulled smoothly into place. If this exchange of linen is accomplished skillfully, the guest need not be disturbed unduly during the procedure. Soiled linen should be properly disposed of immediately after it is removed from the table.

Serving Multiple Tables

Once your servers master how to wait on one table, they need to learn how to wait on multiple tables. Let's say a server is responsible for three tables. The first two tables are seated at the same time. The server brings water to both of these tables. Then the server should take a drinks order from each table. By the time the server returns with the drinks, the host has seated the third table. The server should stay with the first two tables and see if they're ready to order. If they are, the server should then take the order, swing by and get a drink order from Table 3. Next, he or she should take the food order from Tables 1 and 2 to the kitchen. After the server drops this off, he or she will return with Table 3's beverages and see if they are ready to order. If you see that a server is "in the woods," help the server or get the host or hostess or a busser to help.

Fast Fact

Excellent service becomes impossible when a server is responsible for too many tables. Try to limit each server to four or five.

Tips for Serving Customers

Approach the table	• Smile and warmly greet the customer. • Introduce yourself and be courteous.
Get guests settled	• Help with any additional seating such as highchairs and booster chairs. • Remove extra place settings. • Help any guests with disabilities. • Present guests with menus from the right side using your right hand.
Take drink order	• Ask guests if they would like to start with a drink. • Make sure to get all the details of drink orders, such as whether guests want drink on the rock or up, and check on garnishes. • Pay special attention to children, getting their drink order and seeing if the customer would like for the children to be served right away.
Serve drinks	• Place a beverage napkin in front of the guest. • Serve all drinks from the right and place on the beverage napkin.
Tell about specials	• When you bring the initial drink order, tell the guests about any specials, describing preparation methods, ingredients and price.

Check back for second drink order and appetizer order	• If second drinks are ordered, remove the first glasses and napkins. • Refill any wine glasses if guests are sharing a bottle of wine. • Ask the guests if they have any questions about the menu or specials. • Ask if guests would like an appetizer or salad to start their meals.
Take food order	• Ask guests if they are ready to order. Take orders, beginning with the women at the table, if possible. • Suggest salads or side dishes that might be appropriate with entrée selections. • Make sure to collect all the information you need, such as doneness on meat selections and choice of side dishes. • Use correct abbreviations when filling out the guest checks. • When taking the order, be sure to move around the table so you can speak to each guest one on one. • Continue to take the orders in a clockwise pattern around the table. • Collect the menus. • Tidy up the table as needed.
Meeting special requests	• Make sure you know the menu and are able to suggest alternatives to guests with allergies and dietary restrictions, etc. • Write all special requests on your guest check clearly, and make sure to communicate the information to the cooks verbally as well.

	• Check with kitchen staff on ingredient questions and to ensure particular substitutions can be made.
Deliver salads and appetizers	• Provide extra plates if guests are sharing an appetizer plate. • Provide any sauces or accompaniments that come with appetizers. • Ask if guests would like freshly ground pepper on their salads.
Pre-ring food order and place order with kitchen	• Before handing the check back to the kitchen, ring up all items ordered on the computerized cash register or point-of-sale system. • Place order in appropriate spot for the cooks to pick it up (you may need to communicate verbally with the cooks to let them know an order is up). • Make sure you time your orders appropriately. Turn in orders for the next course when guests are about three-quarters of the way through the current course (if the kitchen is busy, you will want to turn in orders sooner than this).
Picking up food	• Collect all the needed serving equipment and cold accompaniments, such as bread, crackers, relishes, butter and cream. • Pick up cold foods next, taking care to keep them away from hot food on the tray. • The hot food should be picked up last. Cover soup to retain the heat. Cover the dinner plate with a hot lid when one is available.

- If hot breads are served, pick them up last to serve them in their best condition.
- When bowl or platter service is used, provide heated plates for hot foods and chilled plates for salads and other cold foods.
- Rinse tea and coffee pots with hot water before filling them with hot beverages. Never pour iced drinks into warm glasses or place butter on a warm plate.
- While waiting for order, be sure to check back with table to see if they need drinks or anything else.
- If an order is taking longer than you expected, check with the head chef or kitchen manager about the delay.
- If food is delayed, do not let guests wait with no explanation. If the manager approves and the delay is significant, you can offer the guests a free beverage or appetizer as you apologize for the delay.
- If you are too busy to pick up an order when it is ready, seek assistance from another server, a bus person, the host or hostess, or manager.
- Check all orders before delivering them to the table to ensure they are correct.
- Make sure plates are attractive (with no smudges or splattered sauces), all garnishes are on the plates, and the temperature is correct (hot foods are hot and cold foods are cold).

Loading the tray	• Put heavier dinner plates and dishes in the center and the lighter pieces toward the edges. Cups are not placed on saucers. • Hot and cold dishes should not touch. • Tea and coffee pots are not filled so full that liquid will leak from the spouts. • Pot spouts are turned in and away from plates or food. • A tray should be loaded so that it will be evenly balanced and the objects on it will neither slip nor spill while it is being carried. Be sure the tray is clean. • Before leaving a serving station, check the order to see that it is correct, complete, properly cooked, the right quantity for serving, properly garnished and attractively served, with no spilled food on the edges of dishes. • Before leaving the kitchen, check to see that all food and the necessary serving equipment for the course are on the tray.
Clear dishes and prepare table for serving	• After any course, dishes should be removed from the left side, except the beverage service which should be removed from the right (do not stack dirty dishes in front of customers). • Place steak knives at the guests place settings, if required. • Bring any condiments the guests might need, making sure the bottles are full. • Check with guests to see if they would like another beverage with their meal.

Delivering food	• Use a tray covered with a clean napkin to carry more than two entrées. • Serve children first, then women, then men. • Serve food from the guest's left with your left hand when possible, but do not reach over customers. • Place the entrée plate so the main item is closest to the customer. • Place side dishes to the left of the entrée plate. • Ask guests if they need anything else. • Remove dirty plates from previous courses as well as empty glasses, and provide clean ashtray if appropriate.
Dessert	• When clearing dinner dishes, ask if guests would like coffee and/or if they would like to see the dessert menu or dessert cart. • Be ready to describe desserts to guests, and suggest that they might want to share one. • Bring coffee orders with cream and sugar. • Bring dessert orders (with extra plates and forks if guests are sharing). • Bring coffee refills.
Clearing table	• Platters and other serving dishes should be removed first when clearing the table, or they may be removed as soon as empty.

- The main-course plate should be removed first, the salad plate next, followed by the bread-and-butter plate.
- The empty milk or beverage glass is removed from the right after the main course.
- The table should be crumbed by using a small plate and a clean, folded napkin. This is especially important when hard rolls or crusty breads are served.
- Hot tea and coffee service should be left on the table until the completion of the dessert course.
- The water glass should remain on the table and be kept refilled as long as the guest is seated.
- Replace soiled ashtrays with clean ones as often as necessary throughout the meal.
- When a guest is seated at a table and it is necessary to change a soiled tablecloth, turn the soiled cloth halfway back, lay the clean cloth half open in front of the guest, and transfer the tableware to the clean cloth. The soiled cloth may then be drawn from the table and the clean one pulled smoothly into place. If this exchange of linen is accomplished skillfully, the guest need not be disturbed unduly during the procedure. Soiled linen should be properly disposed of immediately after it is removed from the table.

| Paying Check | <ul><li>Present the bill in a guest check folder, and tell the guest you will take it when they are ready.</li><li>Resolve any questions or discrepancies on the bill.</li><li>If the guest is paying with cash, present the change in a guest check folder.</li><li>Do not take the tip from the table until the guest leaves.</li><li>If the guest is using a credit card, run the credit card for approval. If the card is denied, politely ask the guest for another card or if they would refer to pay in cash. When returning after the approval has cleared, make sure to bring a pen for the guest's convenience. Also make sure the guest has signed the credit card receipt and left the restaurant's copy.</li><li>Thank the guest when returning with the receipt and/or change and invite them back.</li><li>Inform management or security if a guest leaves without paying.</li></ul> |

Chapter 6
Carrying Trays

Cue the circus music. Carrying trays is a large part of your servers' job, and there are right and wrong ways to go about it. The right ways are safe, hygienic, and efficient. The wrong ways can leave a mess of food on the floor. There are several principles you will want your servers to keep in mind when training on this subject.

Food Trays

If your server is carrying a large tray, he or she should set it down on a tray jack to serve. It is easy enough to serve from a small tray, but serving becomes a hazard if waitstaff tries to hold a heavy tray and serve from it. Another option is to have a second server tail the first one and hold the tray while the original waitperson serves from it.

Loading Trays

Load food trays with the heaviest entrée nearest to your body so that you can use your body to help balance. Also be sure your servers are balancing the entrées on the tray. Plates that are going out to the dining room for service should never be stacked; if the server needs two trays, have them use two trays.

When a waitperson loads his tray, he puts the larger, heavier dinner plates and dishes in the center and the lighter pieces toward the edges. Cups are not placed on saucers. Hot and cold dishes do not touch. Tea and coffee pots are not filled so full that liquid will leak from the spouts. Pot spouts are turned in and away from plates or food.

 **Fast Fact**

A tray should be loaded so that it will be evenly balanced and the objects on it will neither slip nor spill while it is being carried.

Before leaving a serving station, check the order to see that it is correct, complete, properly cooked, the right quantity for serving, properly garnished, and attractively served, with no spilled food on the edges of dishes. Before leaving the kitchen, check to see that all food and the necessary serving equipment for the course are on the tray.

Among the precautions to take in loading a tray are the following:

- Check that the tray is clean.

- Load heavier items in the center of the tray.

- When stacking dishes with covers, don't stack more than four high.

- Don't overload the tray.

- If carrying a large tray, set it down on a tray jack to serve.

- Cocktail trays should be loaded with the heaviest drink in the center to balance the tray.

- Handles should face outward so that the server can easily grasp the cup or glass.

- If carrying food or drinks without trays, only do it for small parties so that all the food can go out at once.

Cocktail Trays

Cocktail trays should be loaded with the heaviest drink in the center to balance the tray. Handles should face outward so that the server can easily grasp the cup or glass.

Arm Service

Many servers carry food or drinks without trays. This should only be done for small parties so that all the food can go out at once. If the party is large enough to require two trips using arm service, the server should use a tray. Servers should be able to carry four plates (three on the right hand and arm and one on the left), or three glasses or two cups and saucers.

Bussing

When using trays for bussing, make sure that your servers stack "like" plates in neat stacks. They should do this as quietly as possible in the dining room.

 **Fast Fact**

Serving staff should not scrape the plates while still in the dining room; this is unappetizing and can disturb customers.

Chapter 7

Suggestions and Suggestive Selling

Some customers come into a restaurant dead set on what they want to order. They've been here before, they know the deal, they want that chicken thing they had last time. But sometimes the customer is adventurous. They may want to explore the far reaches of the menu, they may ask about the day's specials, or they may be open to suggestions before making that big decision. The server who is well-informed and intelligent can be of real service to this sort of guest and at the same time advertise and sell food effectively for the restaurant. This is an opportunity for the waitstaff to be more than an order-takers and servers; they can be successful salespersons as well.

Before the server is ready to take an order intelligently, he must have studied the menu and be familiar with the day's specials and the choices of foods offered on the selective menu. When a foreign name or an uncommon term is used in describing any product, he should be able to pronounce the name correctly and to know what it means in terms of the method of preparation or the manner of service. Some guest is sure to ask for such information about the product. It is annoying to the guest if he cannot answer promptly and must take time to ask someone else.

 **Fast Fact**

Consumers are 68 percent more likely to eat at a restaurant that offers locally produced food.[4]

The server should not only know how a product is prepared and served, but he should also know how it tastes. Many progressive restaurants demonstrate new dishes and specialties to their servers before the serving period begins so that they may taste as well as see the food before they sell it. When the server is asked if something is good, his reply will be much more effective if he can say truthfully: "Yes, I enjoyed it very much" or "I think it is delicious."

Suggesting Selections to the Customer

When a customer is unfamiliar with the restaurant, is hesitant about his food choice or confused about where to find certain items on the menu, the server has a real opportunity to be helpful by offering suitable suggestions. He should be tactful in offering these suggestions and should use intelligence about their form and timing. For example:

- A vegetable plate or a salad and sandwich combination may be suggested when a guest says that she "wants something light."

4. The National Restaurant Organization, 2016

- The "mixed grill special" may be suggested to a guest who can't find a meat that appeals to him on the regular dinner menu.

- The server may suggest that "the fried chicken is very nice" or "the baked ham is especially good" to an uncertain diner who is having difficulty making a selection.

- The server should be able to assist the customer, if necessary, to improve the nutritional value and palatability of the meal. He may suggest a fresh vegetable or a salad when a man orders a meat and potato combination. He may recommend a sherbet or fresh fruit rather than a rich dessert when a customer has had roast pork for the main course and asks him to suggest a dessert.

- The guest may be tempted by the roast lamb offered on the table d'hôte dinner menu, but feels that he cannot afford to pay so much. The server may suggest that roast lamb also is available on a "dinner special" without a first course or dessert, at a lesser price.

Fast Fact

Tact and discretion must be used when making suggestions to customers. The customer should feel that he is being favored by the suggestion and not being forced to buy. When a server's suggestion is not accepted by the guest, the server should in no way show annoyance or disappointment.

The guest may be influenced to give a more complete order than he would otherwise through suggestions made by the server. For instance:

- When the customer orders a sandwich or a salad, the server may ask, "Which do you prefer to drink: tea, coffee, or milk?" thus influencing the customer to add a beverage to his original order.

- When the customer orders a grilled food which must be cooked to order, the server may first tell the customer the time required and then ask if he would like an appetizer or a soup.

- When an a la carte order for a meat course has been served, he may return to the table, present the opened menu and ask, "Would you like to select a dessert?" Another form of suggestion is to name an attractive dessert such as, "The chocolate, pie is very good." or "We have fresh peach ice cream today."

Making Substitutions

Should the guest ask for a substitution on the regular menu, a half-portion or a special service, the server should be sure that such service is permitted before he promises it. If there is any doubt about the matter it should be referred to the hostess or manager for decision.

Purposes of Suggestive Selling

Restaurant customers may be grouped into two categories: those who know what they want to order, and those who are undecided. Indecision may be due to unfamiliarity with the restaurant, difficulty in interpreting the menu, a lack of appetite, or a limited budget. In each case the server may help the customer, either by giving information or by making suggestions.

✗ Fast Fact

Whenever a server prompts a customer to order something which he probably would not have ordered otherwise, she is using suggestive salesmanship.

Meeting the needs of the customer

The best kind of suggestive selling is that which is based on knowledge of the customer's likes and dislikes. This type of selling is particularly applicable to the regular customer. The server should endeavor to learn the customer's preferences in order that she may make suggestions that will be pleasing.

For example, the server may suggest an oyster stew to a tired, chilled motorist; a warm meal to the hungry industrial worker; a salad and sandwich plate to a shopper. When the restaurant is located near the sea, the server may suggest seafood to travelers. The suggestion of foods that are typical of any geographical region is usually appreciated by the visitor to the region.

The server should consider the amount the customer wishes to pay when making suggestions about food selection. She should try to adapt her suggestions to the general price level the customer can afford in order to complete a sale that probably will be satisfactory to him.

 ## Fast Fact

Consumers are 60 percent more likely to eat at a restaurant that offers eco-friendly food.[5]

If the customer signifies that he is willing to spend $20 for his dinner, then an effort should be made to sell him a meal at that price. On the other hand, if the customer indicates that he wishes to limit his expenditure to $10 or less, the server should help him find a satisfactory selection at that price.

The server may make suggestions that will help the customer to meet his nutritional requirements. When the customer tells the server about his dietary restrictions or asks for suggestions for a well-balanced meal, she may suggest articles of food and combinations on the menu, which best meet his needs. For example:

- Suggest fresh fruit when sweet desserts are banned or sugar is rationed.

- Suggest French dressing instead of mayonnaise, or ice cream instead of custard, when eggs are not allowed.

- Suggest consommé instead of cream soup and roast chicken in place of chicken a la king, when the customer has a dairy allergy.

- When wheat products are eliminated from the customer's diet, the server should carefully avoid serving meat with gravy, except natural, unthickened meat juice, and should substitute rye wafers or bread for wheat-flour breads; and a baked apple, a

5. The National Restaurant Organization, 2016

fruit sherbet or a dish of fresh fruit for the pie or cake on the menu.

- When the customer is counting calories, the server may be helpful by suggesting low-calorie foods that are appealing.

Suggesting Additional Items

The server may suggest additional items to the customer, which increase the size of the order. The purpose of such suggestions should be to help the customer make a satisfactory selection, and, at the same time, to sell additional food. This type of suggestive selling may be used to advantage when the customer is ordering from an a la carte menu.

For instance:

- Suggest a beverage with an order for a salad or dessert.
- Suggest a sandwich with an order for a soup or a milk shake.

- Suggest a soup, cocktail or some other "beginner" with an order for grilled or fried food that must be cooked to order.

- Suggest a vegetable or a salad with an order for meat and potatoes.

- A customer who has ordered a main course combination that does not include dessert may be encouraged to order dessert. If the server suggests, "We have fresh Georgia peach shortcake today." or "The Colorado cantaloupe is very good." The presentation of the menu and the inquiry, "What would you like for dessert?" may initiate a sale, whereas the question, "Would you like something else?" probably will elicit a negative reply.

Promoting specials

Before you can suggest a special, you must be familiar with what the special is. Ask your chef or manager for a detailed description before the shift begins, perhaps they could even offer a tasting so you can better describe the special to the customers.

Restaurants offer specials for various reasons. Focus on these reasons when selling them to your customers:

- Specials are made from local ingredients.

- Specials are made from seasonal ingredients.

- Specials offer a better price value.

- Specials are smaller portions.

- Specials are items that aren't usually on the menu.

- Specials are items the restaurant is trying out before putting on the menu.

Suggesting Higher-Priced Items

The food or menu suggested by the server may be more expensive than the one the customer otherwise would have chosen. In this case, as when suggesting additional items, the server should consider the customer's desires and satisfaction more important than the amount of the sale. Higher-priced items may be suggested by the server when:

The customer is uncertain about his selection, and remarks that a chicken sandwich is all he sees that appeals to him, the salesperson may suggest that the customer might enjoy a club sandwich made with chicken, describing how it is made. If this suggestion results in the sale of the club sandwich, the size of the check is increased and the customer may be better nourished as well as better pleased because he has had a well-planned dinner.

Timing of suggestions

Menu suggestions should be made at an appropriate time. For example:

- Make suggestions for the meal selection when the customer is undecided about his initial choice or gives an order for an incomplete course or meal.

- Suggest a dessert just before the customer finishes the main course. At a cafeteria serving counter, alert salespersons may suggest articles of food displayed at any section of the counter.

Particular attention to timing is illustrated by the suggestion of hot rolls as the customer comes to the bread unit or a beverage as he approaches the beverage section.

✕ Fast Fact

Servers should have a thorough knowledge of the day's menu and the specialties of the establishment in order to make good suggestions.

Suggestions should be positive rather than negative. Asked the question, "Will that be all?" just as he has completed the main course, a customer will ordinarily reply, "Yes." "Would you like to order a dessert now?" on the other hand, is positive and will likely be answered in the affirmative.

When an article that has been chosen is "out," the server should know that the supply is exhausted, tactfully explain the shortage to the customer, and suggest something else that may be equally pleasing to him. First, however, the server must try to overcome the guest's disappointment that the article he chose is not available. By expressing regret that there are no fresh strawberries left, and by suggesting that the fresh raspberries are delicious, the server may succeed in selling a substitute and in maintaining the customer's goodwill.

The phraseology a server uses to describe a food may interest the customer and create a desire for the product. Words such as "new," "green," "fresh" "crisp," used in describing fresh vegetables or fruits, indicating as they do an early season or a superior product, enhance their appeal. Terms, which indicate quality or palatability such as "hot" rolls, "chilled" watermelon and "old-fashioned" strawberry shortcake create a mental impression of delicacy, which may help to sell the product.

Success in suggestive selling depends to a large degree upon the interest the food server exhibits when making the suggestion to the customer, and the sincere enthusiasm she expresses for the quality of the suggested product.

Value-Added Service

How do you ensure that first-time customers become repeat patrons? The answer is simple: offer exceptional service. There are certain behaviors that servers should engage in to give good service, then there are behaviors that transform adequate service into value-added service. Many of the devices servers use to increase their tips are also devices that help you increase sales and profits. Encourage your servers to use some of these ploys:

Make recommendations

If, for instance, a customer can't decide on an entrée or a wine, make sure your servers offer recommendations. For example, a server could say, "I tried the halibut special and it was divine!" Making suggestions can be very intuitive. Teach your servers to look for clues about what type of dining experience the patrons are after. Does it seem like a special occasion? If so, customers are more likely to order appetizers and desserts. Do they seem to be on a budget? Then suggest a mid or lower-priced entrée. Remember, these are all suggestions; don't let the servers become pushy.

Remember guests' likes and dislikes

Everyone likes to be remembered. If you have regular customers, encourage your servers to remember their specific food likes and dislikes. For example, if a couple comes in and always orders the same wine, have it ready for them next time before they ask for it. It's guaranteed to charm. It's likely that if they were going to order something different that evening, they will take "the usual" because they appreciate the server remembering their preference.

Be willing to customize

If a customer asks for the steak without sauce, say "No problem!" If the customer wants to substitute rice for potatoes, do so without making a big fuss, checking with the kitchen, or checking with the manager. Let your employees know ahead of time what they can offer without checking with someone. It will reflect on the server and you more positively if the server doesn't have to go and get permission for everything the customer wants!

Go beyond the call of duty

Make the experience of dining at your restaurant unforgettable. Call a cab for the customer and offer a free beverage if they have a long wait. If it's raining, have someone escort the customer to the cab with an umbrella.

Suggest alternatives

If the kitchen has sold out of a particular dish, or if dietary restrictions do not allow a patron to order a particular dish, servers should offer alternatives. If, for example there is a dairy product in the mashed potatoes and the guest is lactose intolerant, the server could suggest, "Our roasted potatoes are made with olive oil; perhaps you would like to substitute those?"

Single diners

Single diners are often uncomfortable dining out. Unfortunately, servers can add to this discomfort by ignoring them. Make sure your servers pay attention to these single diners. Lone diners, however, often turn out to be businesspeople who are using expense accounts, so the sales and tip potential are high. If the guest seems to want to be left alone, seat him or her in a secluded part of the dining room. If they seem eager to talk, spend a moment chatting. You can also offer a single diner reading material if you think that would make them more comfortable. Have reading materials available, and a staff that knows how to offer them politely.

Reinforce a guest's choice

A couple decides to order a bottle of Merlot and are choosing between wine A and wine B. Compliment their decision. Once a guest has placed an order, make them feel good about it. Tell them the strip flank steak looked excellent tonight or that the salmon just came in today. Don't tell them that the pork is a better choice than the steak! Encourage your guests' food choices. The simple act, on your part, of telling them that you've tasted what they're ordering and it's great, can take away any anxiety they have about making a bad choice.

Make personal recommendations

Tell your guests what *you* like. This is not suggestive selling because it's sincere and therefore won't alienate your guests. Your enthusiasm will be infectious, even if guests don't order what you recommend. It won't bother them that you're excited about what's on the menu.

Bring extra napkins

If the guests order a meal that is particularly messy, such as barbecued ribs or lobster in butter sauce, bring them extra napkins before they ask. You should also provide extra napkins when customers dine with children.

Anticipate needs

Bringing a customer something before they ask is an excellent way to win the customer over. Some servers seem to have a sixth sense about it. If you know a particular brand of scotch is very strong, for example, bring the guest a glass of water with the drink they requested. If you are serving red beans and rice, drop off the Tabasco sauce at the same time.

Coffee refills

Make sure your servers provide coffee refills, but also be sure they ask before they pour. The guest might find it annoying to have the cup refilled without being asked. If a half-filled cup has been sitting for awhile, replace the cup with a fresh one rather than filling the lukewarm one.

Doggie bags

Take an extra moment with the doggie bags. Rather than dropping a box off with the customer to fill, fill containers in the kitchen. Add a little something extra as well, perhaps a couple of pieces of bread or extra sauce. Also make sure you have appropriately sized and shaped containers for leftovers. When the customer arrives home and finds her flourless chocolate torte sideways in a soup container it will not reflect well on the server— or the restaurant. For doggie bag sources, check with your local paper vending company. You also can find doggie bags online at McNairn Packaging: **www.mcnairnpackaging.com.**

Keep an eye on your tables

Even if a server is waiting on another table, he/ she should keep an eye on their other tables. If they see a guest looking around, stop over immediately and ask if there is anything you can get them.

Access for disabled

Make sure that your restaurant is accessible for people with disabilities. If there are steps, consider a ramp at the front door. Also have a table, or several tables, that have enough space to accommodate a wheel chair, comfortably. If someone comes in for dinner who is blind, ask the guest if you can offer their seeing-eye dog some water or something to eat. For information about serving guests with disabilities, visit **https://adata.org/factsheet/ food-service**.

Older guests

Another way to give value-added service is to make special arrangements for older guests. Be sure servers are knowledgeable about the menu's nutritional content. Seat older guests in an area that provides good light for them to read the menu. Also, it's harder for the elderly to get in and out of their chairs, so have a few chairs with arms to make life easier for them. Let them know you did it just for them. Finally, ensure that servers respond to elderly customers with patience and respect. They will certainly appreciate it and tip accordingly!

Adding festivity

Does someone at the table have a birthday? Give your servers ways to make the evening festive for the customers. Some restaurants have special desserts for birthdays and other occasions. Other establishments have the entire staff sing to the individual. Even a simple balloon at a table makes the evening seem a bit more festive.

Special requests

Patrons will have special requests for various reasons. A customer may hate the taste of goat cheese and request a different type of cheese on their vegetarian sandwich. Some customers may also have special diets or food allergies with which to contend. A restaurant that doesn't make a big fuss over substitutions can easily win the more restricted or finicky diner's heart!

✕ Fast Fact

Seventy percent of consumers say they prefer ordering healthier food options than they did two years ago.[6]

Hooks for purses and coats

If you don't have a coatroom, add hooks to booths for coats and purses, or provide coat trees in the lobby area.

Calculators with the check

You may want to have a mini calculator attached to your change trays or folders. This will help customers figure out how to split bills and figure tips, without taxing their brains! If they've just enjoyed a relaxing dinner, your guests will appreciate the effort to keep them in that frame of mind!

6. The National Restaurant Organization, 2016

Business customers

Have your servers go the extra length for your business customers. Offer these guests quick service. You can also provide them with some additional services, such as copying, use of the phone and pads of paper and pens for making notes.

Umbrellas when it rains

Is it possible that, given the weather patterns in your area, your guests could arrive without an umbrella, only to find it raining as they're leaving? Offer them umbrellas to help them get to their cars or offices. This could be a great incentive to have them come back at a later date to return the umbrella. Put your name and logo on the umbrella, and maybe it's not the worst thing if they forget to bring it back!

Owner or manager on the floor

People like to meet the person in charge. They appreciate that someone important is checking on them.

Giving directions to guests

Always have a good map on hand. And when guests ask for directions to your restaurant, offer to fax, email, or text the directions to them. If they prefer to speak over the phone, make sure you can give them directions that are easy to understand. Most people will search for directions online before calling your store, so make sure your address is easy to find on your website and social media pages, too.

House camera

If guests are celebrating but forgot a camera, have an instant camera on hand and snap a few shots for them to take home.

Don't ever think about the tip

Focus your energy on taking care of your guests, making them happy, doing little things that exceed their expectations, and generally making their meals as enjoyable as possible. That's how you will consistently get great tips.

Tell the cooks good news

Just like you need to be sensitive to the mood of your guests, be sensitive to the mood of the kitchen crew. The cooks don't want to hear about things just when they're wrong; pass along good news to them and they will probably make it easier for you to take great care of your guests.

Notice lefties

It's a small thing, but if your guest has moved his water glass and/or silverware to the other side of his plate, serve his drinks from there. He'll appreciate it.

Make your movements invisible

That means move with the speed of the room. Good service is invisible: food and drinks simply arrive without a thought on the customer's part. If the room is quiet, don't buzz around in it. If it's more upbeat, move a little quicker. You'll find fitting in seamlessly with the atmosphere will increase your guest's enjoyment—and it's a great way to stay focused.

Tell guests about specific events at your restaurant and invite them to return

It provides an opportunity to build personal connections. For example, invite guests to return for your rib special on Tuesdays. It's far more effective than just saying, "Thanks. Come again." While you're at it, invite them to sit at your station. You'll be more likely to remember their names and what they like.

Chapter 8
Take Care of the Kids

Think back to when you were a kid. Where was your favorite place to eat? It probably had less to do with the food than it did with the atmosphere, the toys that came with the meal, the playground outside, or the games and coloring books on the table.

More and more restaurant owners are realizing the importance of kid-appeal and how it affects where a family decides to eat. Not every restaurant needs a jungle gym necessarily, but children tell their parents when they enjoy a restaurant, and this is as good as a five-star review.

To gain the loyalty of children and their families, you must create a kid-friendly environment. Your servers play a big role in making an establishment kid-friendly, but so do you. Give your servers tools they can use to attain this goal. Here are some suggestions:

Speedy Service

Getting food to the table quickly is key when you're dealing with hungry kids. If it looks like the order might take a while, make sure your staff serves drinks and something to munch on during the wait.

Kid-Friendly Menus

Provide kids with crayons and fun menus to color at the table. Menus should be bright and interesting to look at. They can have blank spaces to draw, comic strips, puzzles, games, and pictures of menu items.

Of course, the most important thing about the kids' menu is the food. Simple and easy to recognize meals and appetizers are essential, but don't hesitate to include smaller portions of adult menu items. Including a drink with each item is also a good way to keep things simple for the parents.

Healthy Choices

This is less about making kids happy than it is about making parents happy. Kids might prefer pizza and potato chips for every meal, but parents will appreciate a menu that offers healthier options. With nutritiously prepared items like fish, chicken, fruits, vegetables, and whole grains on your menu, you will keep your families healthy and happy.

 **Fast Fact**

Research from the National Restaurant Association found that one of the top trends for restaurant menus in 2016 was healthier options for kids.

Kids' Specials

Another excellent way to attract families to your restaurant is to have special times when kids are served at reduced prices. There are many ways you can do this. Online and in-print coupons are often quick and easy options for parents. And a school-related gift certificate program is a fun way to involve the kids. You could even have one day a week when kids under 13 eat free.

Dining out can get pretty expensive for large families. If you go out of your way to make things a little easier on parents' wallets, they will keep coming back.

Kid-Friendly Cups

To help avoid spills and wet clothes, make sure you have small kid-friendly cups on hand. These cups can range anywhere from simple paper cups to colorful plastic cups that match the kids' menu.

Games and Play Spaces

Never miss an opportunity to entertain your customer's kids before, during, and after the meal. Some restaurants are suited to have mini-playgrounds with slides, tunnels, and bridges, but no matter what kind of establishment you have, there is always room for some sort of play space.

The waiting area is a fantastic spot to start. If this is nothing but a nook with a few chairs, consider adding a small table with bead mazes, books, drawing materials, and other toys that can keep kids happy while the family is waiting to be seated. Smaller games at the customer's table will also keep hungry kids in good spirits.

Talk to the Kids

Train your servers to talk to the kids as well as the adults. Granted, your servers aren't baby-sitters, but anything they can do to help the parents and entertain the kids will be welcomed by your guests. Your servers should also be familiar with the kids' menu so they can make suggestions and answer any questions the kids might have.

Paying attention to kids not only helps their parents, but it helps your other customers as well, since an occupied child is less likely to be a screaming child.

Seats

Your regular dining room chairs aren't going to cut it when dealing with little ones, so make sure you have plenty of high chairs, booster seats, and car-seat stands in an easily accessible place. If possible, place these chairs at the table before the party is seated so parents aren't left standing around holding their kids. And if a family has a stroller, try to seat them at a table with plenty of floor space.

Keep an Eye out for Messes

Kids can be chaotic eaters no matter how old they are. Be sure your servers check on family tables often so they can help clean up any accidental spills or messes.

Changing Stations

This is a simple one. Parents with small children expect to find changing stations in most restrooms. Don't let your restaurant be the one that sends them to the parking lot.

Step Stools

If the sinks in your restrooms are too high for small children to reach, put a step stool nearby so they can wash their hands by themselves. This will make the restroom experience a lot easier for them and their parents.

Chapter 9
Server Side-Work Duties

The tasks performed by the waitstaff that aren't related to serving of food are commonly called "side-work duties." These are usually the most monotonous and menial duties of the day, but that doesn't mean they're easy to do or distribute. Each task can take anywhere from 10 minutes to several hours, so schedule things carefully and assign each employee a fair amount of work. Side-work duties are usually done during the slack periods before and after serving hours. These tasks will vary depending on the restaurant, but here are a few examples to keep in mind:

1. Sugar bowls should be kept spotlessly clean: emptied, washed, thoroughly dried and refilled as often as necessary. Care should be taken to keep the sugar free from lumps and foreign material. If shaker-type containers are used, the screw tops should be securely fastened and the spout examined to see if it is clean and that the sugar flows freely.

2. Salt and pepper shakers should be washed with a bottlebrush. A piece of wire or a toothpick may be used to unclog the holes in the lids before they are washed. Shakers should not be filled after washing until they are thoroughly dry. An empty saltbox with a spout may be refilled with pepper and used for filling pepper shakers.

3. Syrup jugs and oil and vinegar containers should always be clean. The outside should be wiped carefully with a damp cloth after filling, to remove any stickiness.

4. Condiment bottles should be wiped with a clean, damp cloth. The top and inside of the cap may be wiped with a paper napkin to clean off gummy material. Mustard pots and condiment jars should be emptied and washed frequently. Clean paddles should be provided often.

5. Napkins should be folded carefully according to the instructions of the restaurant. The folds should be straight and the edges should meet evenly.

6. The appropriate menu for the meal should be used and any special lists and "clip-ons" properly attached. Soiled and torn folders always should be replaced with new ones.

7. When arranging fresh flowers, select containers that are appropriate in color, size and shape for the type of flowers. Arrange the flowers in each vase attractively without overcrowding them.

8. When rearranging flowers, first remove wilted blossoms and leaves. Trim the stems with a pair of scissors. Use cold water for refilling the vases. Carefully dry the outside of the vase before replacing it on the table.

9. The creamers should be washed and thoroughly cooled before being filled with cream.

10. A container with a slender spout may be used for filling individual creamers if a cream dispenser is not available. Care should be taken not to fill the creamers to overflowing.

11. Ashtrays should be collected and cleaned frequently. A small brush may be used to clean caked ashes from the crevices. (As far as possible, ashtrays should be washed separately from other dishes to prevent ashes adhering to them.)

12. Ashtrays should be emptied as often as necessary during the serving period. A clean dish should be provided each time newly arrived guests are seated at a table.

13. The edges and bottoms of serving trays should be kept clean and dry, to protect both the uniform and the serving table surface. The top of the tray should be wiped clean before it is loaded to prevent the bottoms of the dishes from being soiled.

14. Ice cubes and cracked ice should not be used in beverages and drinking water unless they are clean and free from foreign material. Ice cubes should be handled with tongs and cracked ice with a special scoop or serving spoon provided for that purpose.

15. Hands should be washed thoroughly before handling butter. The brick of butter should be placed in the machine in such a way that it can be sliced evenly and without waste. The gauge on the machine should be adjusted properly in order to obtain the right number of pieces of butter. Chilled equipment and a pan of ice should be made ready for handling the butter after it has been cut. Crumbled bits of butter should be saved for use in the kitchen.

16. Crumbs should be dusted from the chair seats after each guest has left the table and before another guest is seated. Backs, rounds and legs of chairs should be carefully dusted every day.

17. Silver should be cleaned according to the special directions of the restaurant.

18. Silver should be cleaned according to the special directions of the restaurant.

Setting Up Coffee Service

- Make sure coffee machines, iced tea containers and coffee thermos containers are clean.

- Stock coffee (regular and decaf) and coffee filters.

- Make two containers of regular coffee and one of decaf ten minutes before the restaurant opens.

- Cut lemons for iced tea.

- Restock sugar, sugar substitute and creamers.

Setting Up Bread Baskets

- Slice enough bread for first seating.

- Prepare bread baskets (line baskets with napkin, then place two or four slices of bread and butter pats in the basket.

Handling Customer Complaints

One of the most difficult duties of the restaurant host is to receive complaints from customers and make satisfactory adjustments. When complaints are properly handled, the customer leaves the restaurant with a feeling of friendliness rather than animosity toward the management. Customer complaints are an opportunity to turn the situation around and make a lifelong customer. Complaints that are improperly handled make the customer disgruntled and may lead to the loss of patronage and unfavorable advertising for the restaurant.

✖ Fast Fact

According to a survey by the Strategic Planning Institute, seven out of 10 customers who complain will return to a business if their complaint is handled properly, and 19 out of 20 will return if their complaint is also handled quickly.

In adjusting complaints, the host should:

1. Approach the customer in a friendly spirit and not allow her to be put on the defensive.

2. Listen attentively to the complaint and try to get the entire story.

3. Restate the gist of the complaint and have the customer confirm this summarized statement.

4. Express sincere regret for the occurrence.

5. Offer to exchange or substitute food that is unsatisfactory.

6. Cite the restaurant's policies when relevant.

7. When the refusal of a request is necessary, explain the reason clearly and tactfully.

8. When the restaurant is at fault, apologize and promise that an effort will be made to prevent a recurrence of the situation.

9. Thank the customer for making the complaint, saying, "I am glad you told me," or "Thank you for bringing this to my attention."

10. When the customer makes a return visit, see that the service is faultless and that she has no further cause for complaint.

11. Refer difficult and unreasonable complaints to the manager for settlement.

12. Report all serious complaints and those involving business policy and regulations to the management.

Dealing with Difficult Customers

Some customers are difficult to deal with because of their attitudes or particular needs; they should be handled with intelligence, tact and good judgment. Different types of customers require different methods of treatment. Here are some examples:

The early customer

Receive him courteously and explain when service will begin. Offer him a comfortable seat, possibly in the lounge, and give him a newspaper or magazine.

The late customer

Make her feel welcome. If the food selection is limited, explain that it's near closing time. Endeavor to provide good service without making her feel that she is being hurried.

The hurried customer

Recommend counter service when this is available. Tell him in advance approximately how long the service will take. Give the best service possible under the circumstances.

The over-familiar customer

Be courteous but dignified with her, avoid long conversations, stay away from the table except when actual service is needed.

The grouchy customer

Meet him cheerfully and see that his waitperson treats him pleasantly. Do not argue with him. Listen to his complaints courteously, but do not encourage him. Do not be distressed by unreasonable complaints.

The angry customer

Listen to her, express regret at the occurrence that prompted her complaint, thank her for calling it to your attention, and try to rectify the error.

The troublemaker

Be courteous but do not be drawn into arguments. Neither participate in criticisms of the management, nor make statements that may be construed as complaints about the restaurant. Warn other salespersons serving the troublemaker type to avoid antagonizing him.

The tired customer

Seat her at a quiet table. Assist her with wraps and packages. In cold weather, suggest a hot soup, a hot drink and some particularly appetizing light food. On a hot day, suggest a chilled salad or a frosted drink.

Remember These Golden Rules:

1. The customer is always right. Make sure this becomes a mantra for your servers. The customer is paying the bill and we as restaurant employees and managers should do everything in our power to see that the guest's experience is positive.

2. Apologize. Before anything else happens, offer a sincere apology for the mistake and offer to fix it.

3. Respond to a problem quickly. By responding to a problem quickly, you prevent it from becoming a crisis. If a wrong order goes out of the kitchen, fix it immediately; don't make the guest wait in line for his correct meal.

4. Make sure you listen to your customer's complaint. Show the guest that you are concerned and sincere in offering your apology. Do something to show that that customer's business is important to you.

5. There are many ways to compensate a customer for a mistake. Taking something off the bill or offering free dessert or a round of drinks are popular methods. If something is spilled on a guest, you should offer to pay the dry cleaning bill. You could also give the guest a free gift certificate for their next meal or send flowers to their workplace or residence. Check with your manager on ways to compensate an unsatisfied customer.

6. Thank the customer for making the complaint, saying, "I am glad that you told me." or "Thank you for bringing this to my attention."

7. When the customer makes a return visit, see that the service is faultless and that he has no further cause for complaint.

8. Refer difficult and unreasonable complaints to the manager for settlement.

9. Report all serious complaints and those involving business policy and regulations to the management.

10. If a customer calls with a complaint, do not keep the customer waiting on hold. Write down the caller's name, address and phone number, and respond to the compliant in a soothing, courteous tone. Apologize for the problem and offer a solution.

Handling Problems

Unfortunately, on occasion things don't go well and a customer has a problem or becomes a problem. The following are a few common problems that might arise and ways to deal with them.

The drunk customer

Excessive alcohol consumption must be controlled in the dining room for the sake of other customers and for the liability to the restaurant and yourself. When a customer has had too much to drink, it is often hard to reason with him or her and the customer can become angry or argumentative very quickly. Do not do anything that would suggest you are being confrontational.

- Try to get the customer to see that you are on their side. Tell the guest that you are concerned for their ability to drive home and you want to see him or her remain safe.

- Try to get the guest to get something to eat. It's a good way to metabolize the alcohol already in the guest's system. If the guest refuses to order, try getting him or her something on the house.

- If a guest refuses to eat and leaves the facility drunk, the restaurant is legally required to notify the police. Let the guest know this and try to get him or her to come back, sit down and eat something.

- If the guest is with a companion, it might make more sense to try to reason with that guest rather than the intoxicated one.

- Be sure to file a report with your manager concerning the incident

- If you are uncomfortable dealing with an intoxicated guest or the situation escalates, be sure to get your manger involved.

The rowdy table

Rowdy tables can be very disruptive to your other customers. The acceptable noise level is partially determined by the type of establishment — people will be much louder in a sport bar than a fine-dining restaurant. If you have a table that is getting out of control, you must make them aware of the situation. Notify your manager or the host of the situation and they will talk with the head of the party and ask them to quiet down. If the guest refuses to cooperate, they will have to be asked to leave.

Pets

The only pet most departments of health will allow in a restaurant are seeing-eye dogs. If a restaurant has an outdoor seating area, however, they will often allow pets there. If someone tries to bring in a pet that is not an assistive animal, tell them that the restaurant does not allow animals and show the owner where the pet can stay while the owner dines. Some restaurants also provide bowls of water and have biscuits on hand for these situations — this can go a long way in keeping your customers happy!

Cellphones

Cellphones are a fact of life. Most of the time people do not turn off these devices when they dine, and most people answer them fairly quickly. Most of the time cellphone conversations will not disturb other guests. If, however, your dining room is quiet and this behavior becomes disruptive to other customers, you should ask the offending party if they would mind taking their calls in the lounge or lobby area.

The well-known guest

Famous people and other well-known personalities often simply want to dine in peace and not be disturbed by someone wanting an autograph or someone wanting to start a conversation. To facilitate this experience, the host should find the guest an out-of-the-way table and assign the table an experienced server who is less likely to be "star struck" by the guest.

Accidents

Accidents, large and small, are bound to happen on your shift. If a small accident happens, such as a spill, it can be easily and quickly dealt with. If you or a customer spills something on the table, quickly move all items to the other side, place a clean napkin on the spill then return all the items to their original positions. If something is spilled on the customer, you should help the guest clean up the spill and apologize. If appropriate, you should also offer to pay for any dry cleaning charge the guest incurs because of the spill.

 **Fast Fact**

A survey by Cintas Corporation found that one in three U.S. adults would be unlikely to eat at a restaurant where someone experienced a slip-and-fall accident. That's around 60 million Americans.[7]

7. Business Wire, 2012

If a more serious accident happens, immediately notify your manager. Your manager can determine whether medical care is necessary. Whatever the accident is, the first thing you should do is attend to the guest. Afterward be sure to follow any policy your restaurant has about logging or recording accidents with an accident report. Be sure you include the name of the guest, your name, the date and time, and a complete description of the incident.

Food poisoning

Every restaurant manager dreads the thought of a call from a customer who has suffered from food poisoning. Every restaurant should have a plan developed for dealing with this situation. Check with your manager and be sure you know what this plan is and what you should do if it occurs.

If a customer calls with a complaint of food poisoning, do not become defensive. Make sure you are sympathetic with the customer, saying you are sorry they were ill.

Record all the facts the restaurant will need to investigate the situation and turn this information over to your manager immediately.

Chapter 10
Menu Knowledge

The food is the most important thing about your restaurant, and your menu is the map that helps your customers find exactly what they want. Servers need to be knowledgeable of this menu so they can answer all of the customers' questions. If the server doesn't take the time to study the menu, the customer may become frustrated (a bad combination when hungry) and decide that the food isn't worth their time either.

✖ Fast Fact

In order to make a satisfactory selection, customers need information about the restaurant's food. Experience with patrons and an ability to anticipate their desires will enable the server to know just how much information he or she should give each customer.

Many questions customers may ask concern the types of products used by the restaurants. The servers need to be informed about the kind, the grade, and source of these food products. Customers may want answers to such questions as:

- Are the peas fresh or frozen?

- Is this local asparagus?

- Are the cantaloupes from California?

- Is the mayonnaise made with olive oil?

- Is the salmon fresh or frozen?

- Is the grapefruit juice sweetened?

- Is the grapefruit from Texas or Florida?

These and many other questions about the food are asked of the server. Although it is not possible to anticipate all of the questions about the food that customers will ask, certain types of inquiries occur commonly enough that they may be forecast.

It is important that servers have this kind of information at the tip of their tongues in order that they may answer as many of these common questions as possible. Servers shouldn't have to keep the customer waiting while they ask someone else, unless that is necessary in order to give an accurate reply. Neither should they bluff nor give guests misleading and inaccurate information, for this will reflect unfavorably upon the business and upon the employee.

Cooking Terms and Methods on Preparation

Customers will also have questions about how menu items are prepared, so servers must be trained on this information as well.

The customer often wants information about how a dish is prepared. The server should be informed concerning the methods of preparing the dishes he or she serves so that the server may give the requested explanation promptly and accurately.

Suppose for instance:

1. The customer asks how imperial crabmeat is prepared. The server might reply that it is fresh crabmeat, combined with cream, capers and minced pepper, and baked in the shell or in a ramekin.

2. The customer asks how "Spanish steak" is prepared. The server might explain that it is braised round steak cooked in and served with tomato sauce.

3. The customer asks what is meant by the term "Creole sauce." The reply should be that it is a sauce made with tomatoes, peppers and onions.

4. The customer is on a special diet and unable to eat certain kinds of food, it is most important to him that the server be able to tell him the ingredients from which a dish is made.

5. Are there onions in the soup? Is the pie thickened with cornstarch? Are the potatoes fried in lard? These and many similar questions are very important to the customer who may, for instance, experience distress when he eats onions, or may be allergic to corn products, or be on a low-fat diet and unable to eat fried foods.

Make sure your servers are schooled in basic cooking terminology. Here are some of the more important terms with which they should be familiar:

Au Gratin: A dish topped with bread crumbs and cheese or sauce, and browned.

Baked/roasted: Cooked in the oven, uncovered.

Blackened: Seasoned with spices including cayenne and cooked over extremely high heat in a heavy skillet.

Braised: Cooked in the oven, covered.

Coulis: A thick pureed sauce.

Deep fried: Food is submerged in hot, liquid fat and thoroughly cooked.

Fried: Cooked in hot fat, usually butter or oil, over medium to high heat.

Grilled: Cooked on a grate over charcoal, wood or gas.

Marinade: A liquid used to flavor food before cooking, can include herbs, spices, lemon, oil or alcoholic beverages.

Poached: Cooked in or over boiling water.

Purée: Ingredient is blended until it reaches a smooth consistency. Many salad dressings and sauces are made with fruit or vegetable purées.

Reduce: To boil a liquid rapidly until evaporation reduces the volume. This intensifies the flavor; it is often a method used for sauces.

Roux: Equal parts of flour and fat cooked over high heat. Used to thicken sauces; most commonly used in Cajun cooking.

Sautéed: Cooked very quickly in a small amount of fat over direct heat.

Seared: Usually refers to meat and means browning quickly by subjecting the item to very high heat.

Steamed: Cooked by placing over a rack or in a steamer basket and then placed over simmering or boiling water in a covered pan.

Stewed: The food is barely covered with a liquid and simmered slowly in a pan with a tightly fitting lid.

Simmered: Food is cooked gently in hot liquid, low enough to keep tiny bubbles breaking on the surface.

Stir-fried: Quickly fried food cut into small pieces over high heat while constantly stirring.

The approximate length of time required to prepare cooked-to-order foods of various kinds should be known by the server as well. A customer who must eat hurriedly should be told that it will take at least ten minutes to prepare and serve a broiled steak order. In this instance, the server may save time for the customer by suggesting that veal steak is available on one of the ready-to-serve dinners or that the prime rib is very good and can be served immediately.

When the customer has been informed that he must wait a given length of time for cook-to-order food, he will probably wait more patiently and more contentedly. Often, he may be open to suggestion about a first course that he may enjoy while waiting for his special order to be prepared.

 ## Fast Fact

The alert server will suggest an appetizer or soup when he or she tells the customer the approximate time required to fill his special order.

Chapter 11
Restaurant Technology

Gone are the days when the only technology a restaurant needed was a cash register and maybe a television or two. Technology is changing every day, and it's changing the way the entire world operates—including restaurants. If you don't adapt, your establishment might score some points with the hipster crowd, but you will eventually fall behind. Technology isn't just about getting the shiniest new gadgets, it's about saving money, increasing efficiency, improving your customers' experience, and getting a leg up on the competition.

✕ Fast Fact

Seventy-Five percent of smartphone users say that they use their devices to look at restaurant menus.[8]

New Technology

Of course, not every restaurant needs to line their walls with the latest gizmos, but it's a good idea to keep an eye out for things that will improve your business. According to a 2016 survey by the National Restaurant Association, 71 percent of restaurants offer free Wi-Fi for their guests, 25 percent offer online reservations, and 49 percent offer online ordering and mobile payment.

8. The National Restaurant Organization, 2016

You can even use the public's smartphone addiction to your advantage. With an official app, you can offer customers quick access to menus, loyalty programs, payment options, nutrition information, and a map to your restaurant.

 **Fast Fact**

According to the National Restaurant Organization, 37 percent of consumers say that technology makes them patronize restaurants more often, and 72 percent say that restaurant technology increases convenience.

Electronic Ordering

While smartphones are introducing exciting new ways for customers to pay for their meals, the touch-screen system—also known as the POS (point-of-sale) system—remains the most widely-used technology in the food service industry to date. The POS system is basically an offshoot of the electronic cash register. These systems were introduced to the food service industry in the mid-1980s and have since made their way into over 80 percent of restaurants nationwide. From fine-dining establishments to fast-food joints, the touch screen is effortless. In fact, a child could be trained to use it in a few minutes. And because of their speed and accessibility, such systems tend to pay for themselves. According to information published by the National Restaurant Association, a restaurant averaging $1,000,000 in food-and-beverage sales can expect to see an estimated savings of $30,000 per year. Understanding the numbers collected by a POS system will give the operator more control over inventory, bar revenues, labor scheduling, overtime, customer traffic and service. Understanding POS data ultimately clarifies the bottom line, knocking guesswork out of the equation.

A point-of-sale system comprises two parts: the hardware (equipment) and the software (the computer program that runs the system). This system allows waitstaff to key in their orders as soon as the customers give them. Additional keys are available for particular options and specifications, such as "rare," "medium-rare" and "well-done." Some systems prompt the waitstaff to ask additional questions when the item is ordered, such as, "Would you like butter, sour cream or chives with the baked potato?" Some will suggest a side dish or a compatible wine.

The order is sent through a cable to printers located throughout the restaurant: at the bar, in the kitchen and the office. All orders must be printed before they are prepared, thus ensuring good control. When a server has completed the ordering, a guest check can be printed and later presented. Most POS systems allow certain discounts and require manager control over others. Charge cards, cash and checks can be processed separately, and then reports can be generated by payment type.

Some benefits of using a POS system:

- Increases sales and accounting information
- Custom tracking
- Reports waitstaff's sales and performance
- Reports menu-item performance
- Reports inventory usage
- Accurate addition on guest checks
- Prevents incorrect items from being ordered
- Prevents confusion in the kitchen
- Reports possible theft of money and inventory
- Records employee timekeeping
- Reports menu-sales breakdown for preparation and menu forecasting
- Reduces time spent walking to the kitchen and bar
- Less distance to travel for the servers
- The waitstaff can always keep the customers within their field of vision

- Ease of processing credit cards

- Because waitstaff are always visible in the dining area, customers are able to easily attract their waitperson's attention

As the labor market continues to diminish, touch screens with POS systems will become necessary. It has been predicted that in the next few years, customers may even place their own orders.; terminals will be simply turned around. During peak seasonal periods, ordering food may be like pumping your own gas; customers will key in their own selections, then slide their credit cards through to pay.

✕ Fast Fact

When surveyed, only 31 percent of consumers said they would be open to text message marketing from a limited-service restaurant.[9]

Many POS systems have been greatly enhanced to include comprehensive home delivery, guest books, online reservations, frequent-diner modules and fully integrated systems with real-time inventory, integrated caller ID, accounting, labor scheduling, payroll, menu analysis, purchasing and receiving, cash management, and reports. Up-and-coming enhancements and add-ons include improved functionality across the internet, centralized functionality enabling "alerts" to be issued to managers, and voice-recognition POS technology.

Handling Money

While keeping your customers happy is an important aspect of your job, accurately collecting payment is as important—without cash, the restaurant can't stay in business!

Whether you are using an electronic ordering system or a hand-written system, one of the most important elements in these systems is the guest

9. The National Restaurant Organization, 2016

check. All information concerning a sale should be recorded on a guest check. Guest checks are used by the server at the time of service to be sure their customers receive everything they order. Management uses guest checks to accumulate numerous types of information, such as how many covers were served on that particular day and how many tables a particular server had. This information allows management to make adjustments to staffing requirements if necessary and helps them find ways to improve service.

Your manager or the cashier will issue guest checks to the servers at the beginning of the shift and collect all unused guests at the end of the shift. A missing check might indicate carelessness or it might indicate theft. When you receive your stack of guest checks for the shift, be sure to go through them to ensure they are all present before starting your shift. Your manager or cashier will also likely have you sign the checks, indicating they are all present and you are taking responsibility for that batch of checks until they are turned in.

Most check checks have three distinct areas: an information box, the body, and the customer's receipt. The information box contains the date, table number and server number or name. It may also include the number of guests at the table, the sequential number of guest check, and the time the order was taken (the sequential number provides a control system that allows management to account for every order). The body of the guest is the area the server uses to record the actual orders, special requests, prices and taxes. The receipt section can be given to the customer for his or her records, and usually includes an area for the total spent and the restaurant's logo and location information.

Writing Orders

When filling out your checks, be sure to write clearly. Many people will need to be able to read these checks including management, the cooking staff, the accountant, the guest, another server that might be helping, and yourself! Also be sure that you are using the correct abbreviations for all items. You should receive a list of abbreviations in your orientation materials.

 **Fast Fact**

Technology can make a restaurant run much smoother, but not everyone sees it that way. According to the National Restaurant Organization, 42 percent of consumers found that new technology made their dining experiences more complicated. When introducing new technology to your establishment, consider having an employee on standby to help explain how to use it.

Presenting the Check

Before presenting the check to the customer, carefully review it to make sure the customer is not being overcharged or undercharged. Be sure all items are listed and prices are correct. If the guest has questions concerning the bill, answer them politely. Be sure to correct any errors quickly and with an apology.

If the guest pays with a personal check, you should follow these steps:

- Check the date on the check.

- Check the amount for which the check is written.

- Make sure it was written as being payable to the restaurant.

- Request the guest's identification.

- Initial the check so when you give it to the cashier he or she knows you've verified the information on the check.

If the guest pays with a credit card and your establishment does not use a POS system, follow these steps:

- Take the guest check and credit card to the cashier station and imprint the card on a charge form.

- Swipe the card through the authorization machine.

- Key in the amount.

- Wait for the authorization number.

- Write the authorization number on the form.

- Make sure all other information has imprinted clearly.

- Fill in the amount of the check and the tax.

- Take the form, guest check and a pen back to the customer for his or her signature.

- Show the guest which copy of the form is the customer's receipt.

If the guest pays with a credit card and your establishment does use a POS system:

- Enter the amount of the check into the authorization machine.

- A slip is printed out with the authorization number.

- Present the slip to the customer (this slip is the same as the manual form and is used for the customer's signature).

- Once the customer has signed, the server enters the exact amount (including gratuity) into the payment system. The funds will be electronically transferred into the restaurant's account.

Remember, a credit card voucher is cash, and if a voucher is lost, the restaurant has lost that venue. Credit card vouchers should be given to the cashier with cash. If you are using manual forms and there are carbons, be sure to destroy these to help protect your customers against fraud.

If the credit card authorization machine declines charges, take the flowing steps:

- Try the card again in case the machine read the card incorrectly.

- If the card is declined a second time and the guest must be asked to provide another form of payment, ask the guest if they have another card they could use because the machine is not reading that card.

- If the guest insists that the card is good, the bank's phone number is on the back, so you could let the guest call the bank to try to straighten out the situation.

On occasion the credit card authorization machine might display the message "call issuer." If this happens, let your manager know. He or she will need to call the card issuer. The issuer may say to keep the card and/or cut it in half. This may happen if the card has been stolen of the account is extremely overdue.

Problems

There are some special money problems that may happen during your shift, and it would be wise to know how to deal with these.

Customer leaves without paying

If you notice a guest leaving before he or she pays, tactfully remind them about the bill—it is entirely possible that they simply forgot. If a customer leaves without paying, do not follow the customer outside to try to get the money. Immediately notify your manager. Your manager will decide whether or not to inform the police.

Guest can't pay

Immediately notify your manager. Most establishments have a policy in place for what to do when this happens.

Robbery

Don't try to be a hero. Often heroics only lead to an escalation of the situation and someone may get hurt. Stay calm and try to remember any details about the robber so you can give the police a good description. Also be sure to know the policy your establishment has on what to do during and after a robbery.

Guest Tickets and the Cashier

There are various methods of controlling cash and guest tickets. The following section will describe an airtight system of checks and balances for controlling cash, tickets and prepared food. Certain modifications may be needed to implement these controls in your own restaurant. Many of the cash registers and POS systems available on the market can eliminate most of the manual work and calculations. The systems described in this section are based on the simplest and least expensive cash register available. The register must have three separate subtotal keys for food, liquor and wine sales, and a grand-total key for the total guest check. Sales tax is then computed on this amount. The register used must also calculate the food, liquor and wine totals for the shift. These are basic functions that most machines have. Guest tickets must be of the type that is divided into two parts. The first section is the heavy paper part listing the menu items. At the bottom is a space for the subtotals, grand total, tax and a tear-away customer receipt. The second section is a carbon copy of the first. The carbon copy is given to the expediter, who then issues it to the cooks, who start the cooking process. Some restaurants utilize handheld ordering computers, and/or the tickets may be printed in the kitchen at the time of entry into the POS system or register. Regardless, the expediter must receive a ticket in order to issue any food.

The tickets must have individual identification numbers printed in sequence on both parts and the tear-away receipt. They must also have a space for the waiter's name, date, table number and the number of people at the table. This information will be used by the expediter and bookkeeper in tracking down lost tickets and/or food items. Each member of the waitstaff is issued a certain number of tickets each shift. These tickets are in numbered sequence.

For example, a waiter may be issued 25 tickets from 007575 to 007600. At the end of the shift, he must return to the cashier the same total number of tickets. No ticket should ever become lost; it is the responsibility of the waitstaff to ensure this. Should there be a mistake on a ticket, the cashier must void out all parts. This ticket must be turned in with the others after being approved and signed by the manager. The manager should issue tickets to each individual waiter and waitress. In certain instances, the manager may approve of giving away menu items at no charge. The manager must also approve of the discarding of food that cannot be served. A ticket must be written to record all of these transactions. Listed below are some examples of these types of situations:

Manager food

All food that is issued free of charge to managers, owners and officers of the company.

Complimentary food

All food issued to a customer compliments of the restaurant. This includes all food given away as part of a promotional campaign.

Housed food

All food of which is not servable, such as spoiled, burned or incorrect orders.

Cashier's report

All of these tickets should be filled out as usual, listing the items and the prices. The cashier should not ring up these tickets, but record them on the cashier report form. Write the word "manager," "complimentary" or "housed" over the top of the ticket.

The manager issues cash drawers, or "bank," to the cashier. The drawers are prepared by the bookkeeper. Inside the cashier drawer is the cashier's report itemizing the breakdown of the money it contains.

The accuracy of the cashier's report is the responsibility of both the cashier and the manager. Upon receiving the cash drawer, the cashier must count the money in the cash drawer with the manager to verify its contents. After verification, the cashier will be responsible for the cash register. The cashier should be the only employee allowed to operate the register.

Each member of the waitstaff will bring his or her guest ticket to the cashier for totaling. The cashier must examine the ticket to ensure:

- All items were charged for.
- All items have the correct price.
- All the bar and wine tabs are included.
- Subtotals and grand total are correct.
- Sales tax is entered correctly.

The cashier is responsible for filling out the charge card forms and ensuring their accuracy (charge-card procedures are described in Chapter 16). The cashier will return the customer's charge card and receipt to the appropriate member of the waitstaff.

At the end of each shift, the cashier must cash out with the manager. List all the cash in the "Cash Out" columns. Enter the breakdown of sales into separate categories. Do not include sales tax. Enter all complimentary, housed and manager amounts. Itemize all checks on back. Itemize each ticket for total sales and total dinner count. Break down and enter all charged sales.

The total amount of cash taken in plus the charge sales must equal the total itemized ticket sales. Itemize all checks on the back of the cashier's report and stamp "FOR DEPOSIT ONLY"; the stamp should include the restaurant's bank name and account number.

Should a customer charge a tip, you may give the waiter or waitress a "cash paid out" from the register. When the payment comes in, you can then deposit the whole amount into your account. Miscellaneous paid-outs are for any items that may need to be purchased throughout the shift. List all paid-outs on the back and staple the receipts to the page.

When everything is checked out and balanced, the sheet must be signed by the cashier and manager. The manager should then deposit all tickets, register tapes, cash, charges and forms into the safe for the bookkeeper the next morning. The cash on hand must equal the register receipt readings.

Getting Orders to the Kitchen

In many restaurants, the server takes the order by hand at the table, goes to the cashier, server area or another convenient place to enter the information into the computer. Then, depending upon the sophistication of the system, the order either goes to the cooks via the computer system or the server hands the guest check to the kitchen. The order is then placed on a wheel or rack. Most guest checks have multiple layers and writing areas; train your servers how to correctly write the guest check for your kitchen. For instance, the check may have a heavy copy and a carbon layer on top, which is divided into two areas by a perforation. Your server keeps the heavy copy, writes the entrée order on the large section of the perforated sheet and the appetizer on the smaller area. When the guest check goes into the back, the line cook and the appetizer cook split the sheet. For seamless order processing, try the following suggestions:

Guest-check shorthand

Even if you're using a computerized register, your servers may still be writing down orders by hand. If you're using a completely computerized system, you still have abbreviations in place for menu items. Make sure your servers memorize these, and if they are writing them by hand for the cooks, make sure the orders are legible!

Examples of abbreviations

Here is a list of some example abbreviations you can use for menu items. When you develop your own system, be careful of repetition and abbreviations that are too similar:

Spag & mt: Spaghetti and meatballs

Fett: Fettuccine Alfredo

Steak w/mush: Steak Hoagie with mushroom sauce

Chic parm: Chicken Parmigiana

Tossed BC: Tossed salad with blue cheese dressing

Ch man: Cheese manicotti

Burger w Let/tom/on: Hamburger, well done, with lettuce, tomato and onion

Guest-check control

You should always have control measures in place for your guest checks. This helps prevent employees from giving away food and drinks. Stress that all food that leaves the kitchen has to have a guest check accompany it whether it is for a customer or an employee.

Accountability

Make your servers responsible for accounting for all the guest checks at the end of the night when they turn these over to the manager on duty. Rather than keeping a stack of guest checks for servers to pick up as they come on duty, have the manager on duty issue guest checks and keep a log of who was issued what. Management can then spot-check on a random basis and make sure that the amounts and payment methods entered on the guest check match what the computer says. Also, be sure to have a policy in place for what happens if checks go missing.

Chapter 12
Tipped Employees

On the surface, tips seem simple enough. If an employee does their job well, the customer gives them extra money for their services. Simple, right? "Nope," says the IRS. One of the biggest payroll challenges that restaurant owners and managers face is getting employees to report and pay taxes on their tips. Complying with the intricacies of the tip-reporting and allocation rules can be difficult and confusing. Because tip tax laws are constantly changing, you can't be too careful in this area. It's a good idea to get assistance from your accountant or attorney.

✗ Fast Fact

When asked about their tipping habits, 50 percent of Americans said they tipped because they felt it was required, and 34 percent tipped in response to great service.[10]

Once you have consulted with your accountant or attorney, you will need to make sure your front-of-the-house employees are trained in this area. You might want to ask your accountant or attorney to make this presentation with you.

The Tip Rate Determination and Education Program

IRS tip agreements

The IRS is continuing its emphasis on a multi-year strategy to increase tax compliance by tipped employees. Originally developed for the food and beverage industry, this program has now been extended to the gaming (casino) and hairstyling industries.

There are three arrangements under this program that, depending on their business, employers in specific industries can agree to enter into: The Tip Rate Determination Agreement (TRDA) is available to the gaming and the food and beverage industries, the Tip Reporting Alternative Commitment (TRAC) is available to the food and beverage and the hairstyling industries, and the Employer-designed Tip Reporting Alternative Commitment (EmTRAC) is available to employers in the food and beverage industries who wish to develop their own TRAC programs.

First introduced in 1993, the TRDA set the stage for a new way of doing business at the IRS. This arrangement emphasizes future compliance by tipped employees in the food and beverage industry by utilizing the tip rates individually calculated for each retail beverage and food outlet. In addition, as long as the participants comply with the terms of the agree-

10. Kalpana, 2013

ment and accurately report their tip income, the IRS agrees not to initiate any examinations during the period the TRDA is in effect.

The second arrangement, TRAC, grew out of a collaborative effort between the IRS and a coalition of restaurant industry representatives. It was first introduced in June 1995. TRAC emphasizes educating both employers and employees to ensure compliance with the tax laws relating to tip income reporting. Employees are provided tip reports detailing the correlation that exists between an employee's charge tip rate and the cash tip rate. In general, the IRS district director will not initiate any examinations on either the employer or employees while the agreement is in effect if participants comply with the provisions of the agreement.

The third arrangement, EmTRAC, was developed in response to food and beverage employers who wished to build their own TRAC programs. This arrangement is available to employers whose employees receive charged tips and cash tips, and it retains most of the TRAC agreement's provisions.

Participation in one of these programs is voluntary, but you may only enter into one of the agreements at a time.

✖ *Fast Fact*

1998 tax legislation specifies that the IRS can't threaten to audit you in order to convince you to sign a TRDA, TRAC, or EmTRAC agreement.

The big benefit for you, as an employer, is that you will not be subject to unplanned tax liabilities. Those who sign these agreements receive a commitment from the IRS that the agency will not examine the owner's books to search for under-withheld or underpaid payroll taxes on tip income. There are benefits to employees, also, including increases in their Social Security, unemployment compensation, retirement plan and workers' compensation benefits.

Under TRDA, the IRS works with you to arrive at a tip rate for your employees. Then at least 75 percent of your tipped workers must agree in writing to report tips at the agreed-upon rate. If they fail to do so, you are required to turn them in to the IRS. If you do not comply, the agreement is terminated and your business becomes subject to IRS auditing.

The TRAC and EmTRAC agreements are less strict, but they require more work on your part. There is no established tip rate, but you are required to work with employees to make sure they understand their tip-reporting obligations. You must set up a process to receive employees' cash tip reports, and they must be informed of the tips you are recording from credit card receipts.

Additional Information on Tip-Reporting

The following IRS forms and publications relating to tip income reporting can be read and downloaded directly from the government website: **www .irs.gov/forms-pubs.** Use the search bar to look up the following:

Pub 505: Tax Withholding and Estimated Tax

Pub 531: Reporting Tip Income

Form 941: Employer's Quarterly Federal Tax Return

Form 4137: Social Security and Medicare Tax on Unreported Tip Income

Form 8027: Employer's Annual Information on Tip Income and Allocated Tips.

Employee Tip-Reporting Frequently Asked Questions

Because you're an employee, the tip income you receive, whether it's cash or included in a charge, is taxable income. As income, these tips are subject to federal income tax and Social Security and Medicare taxes, and may be subject to state income tax as well.

Q: What tips do I have to report?
A: If you received $20 or more in tips in any one month you should report *all* your tips to your employer so that federal income tax, Social Security and Medicare taxes—maybe state income tax, too—can be withheld.

Q: Do I have to report all my tips on my tax return?
A: Yes. All tips are income and should be reported on your tax return.

Q: Is it true that only 8 percent of my total sales must be reported as tips?
A: No. You must report to your employer 100 percent of your tips, except for the tips *totaling* less than $20 in any month. The 8 percent rule only applies to employers.

Q: Do I need to report tips from other employees?
A: Yes. Employees who are indirectly tipped by other employees are required to report "tip-outs." This could apply to bus persons, for instance.

Q: Do I have to report tip-outs that I pay to indirectly tipped employees?
A: If you are a directly tipped employee, you should report to your employer only the amount of tips you retain. Maintain records of tip-outs with your other tip income (cash tips, charged tips, split tips, tip pool).

Q: What records do I need to keep?
A: You must keep a running daily log of all your tip income.

Q: What can happen if I don't keep a record of my tips?
A: Underreporting could result in your owing substantial taxes, penalties and interest to the IRS and possibly other agencies.

Q: If I report all my tips to my employer, do I still have to keep records?
A: Yes. You should keep a daily log of your tips so that, in case of an examination, you can substantiate the actual amount of tips received.

Q: Why should I report my tips to my employer?
A: When you report your tip income to your employer, the employer is required to withhold federal income tax, Social Security and Medicare taxes, and, maybe, state income tax. Tip-reporting may increase your Social Security credits, resulting in greater Social Security benefits when you retire. Tip-reporting may also increase other benefits to which you may become entitled, such as unemployment benefits or retirement benefits.

Additionally, a greater income may improve financing approval for mortgages, car loans and other loans.

Q: I forgot to report my tip income to my employer, but I remembered to record it on my federal income tax return. Will that present a problem?
A: If you do not report your tip income to your employer, but you do report the tip income on your federal income tax return, you may owe a 50 percent Social Security and Medicare tax penalty and be subject to a negligence penalty and, possibly, an estimated tax penalty.

Q: If I report all my tips, but my taxes on the tips are greater than my pay from my employer, how do I pay the remaining taxes?
A: You can either pay the tax when you file your federal income tax return or you can reach into your tip money and give some to your employer to be applied to those owed taxes.

Q: What can happen if I don't report my tips to the IRS?
A: If the IRS determines through an examination that you underreported your tips, you could be subject to additional federal income tax, Social Security and Medicare taxes and, possibly, state income tax. You will also be awarded a penalty of 50 percent of the additional Social Security and Medicare taxes and a negligence penalty of 20 percent of the additional income tax, plus any interest that may apply.

Q: What is my responsibility as an employee under the Tip Rate Determination Agreement (TRDA)?
A: You are required to file your federal tax returns. You must sign a Tipped Employee Participation Agreement, proclaiming that you are participating in the program. To stay a participating employee, you must report tips at or above the tip rate determined by the agreement.

Q: What is my responsibility as an employee under the Tip Reporting Alternative Commitment (TRAC)?
A: For a directly tipped employee, your employer will furnish you a written statement (at least monthly) reflecting your charged tips. You are to verify

or correct this statement, and you are to indicate the amount of cash tips received. When reporting your cash tips, keep in mind that there is a correlation between charged tips and cash tips. You may be asked to provide the name and amount of any tip-outs you've given to indirectly tipped employees. For an indirectly tipped employee, you are required to report all your tips to your employer.

Tips-Reporting Policies

So, who has to report tips? Employees who receive $20 or more in tips per month are required to report their tips to you in writing. When you receive the tip report from your employee, you should use it to figure the amount of Social Security, Medicare and income taxes to withhold for the pay period on both wages and reported tips. (For more information on employer tip-reporting responsibilities, visit the IRS's website at: **www.irs.gov**, and look at Publication 15, Circular E, Employer's Tax Guide. For more information on employee responsibilities, look at Publication 531, Reporting Tip Income.)

Chapter 13
Beverage Service

Alcohol Sales Policies

Selling alcohol not the same as selling a hamburger. Sure, if a restaurant has a wine and beer or liquor license, alcohol sales can be a large source of revenue and tips—just like any other product. Unfortunately, alcohol can also be a bit of a liability as well. Newspapers are full of stories about restaurants and employees being sued because one of their drunk patrons wound up hurting or killing someone. You don't have to worry about that from someone who ate one too many french fries. The first step in responsible alcohol sales is to be sure that you and your servers know the laws and ramifications of the laws that affect the business.

✕ Fast Fact

Alcohol sales tend to be recession-proof. No matter how bad the economy is, most people still find ways to drink.[11]

Know the signs of intoxication

These can include slurred speech, loss of inhibition, aggressiveness, and loss of muscle coordination.

Know your restaurant's alcohol sales policy

This policy should include a description of federal, state and local laws that govern your alcohol sales. It should also lay down a set of rules for your servers, including not selling to minors and intoxicated customers. You should also set limits. For example, put a policy into place that says if a customer has four drinks, the server should notify the manager. The manager can then monitor the situation and determine whether or not the customer needs to be cut off. You may also want to set up a relationship with a local cab company for those occasions when you need to suggest a cab to one of your patrons.

Keep track of customers' intake if it looks like there may be a potential problems. You can also have servers offer a menu to customers who may only be drinking. If necessary, you may want to bring an intoxicated patron a freebie. In the long run, this is much cheaper than a lawsuit!

If an incident happens

Make sure you get management involved in any incident. Also, document everything that occurs.

11. Morley, n.d.

Resources

The International Alliance for Responsible Drinking offers training materials related to responsible beverage-alcohol service. You can find this information at: **www.iard.org**. They also offer numerous free downloads of resources concerning alcohol awareness and a blood alcohol concentration (BAC) calculator.

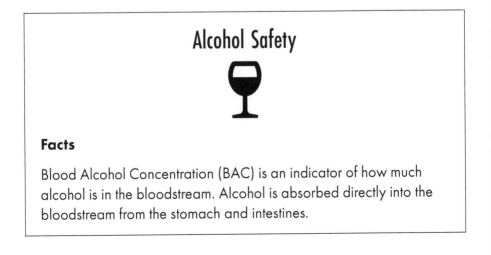

Alcohol Safety

Facts

Blood Alcohol Concentration (BAC) is an indicator of how much alcohol is in the bloodstream. Alcohol is absorbed directly into the bloodstream from the stomach and intestines.

At 0-10 a person is considered legally intoxicated in most states. In our state the level of legal intoxication is _____.

Factors that affect the absorption of alcohol into the bloodstream include:

- Amount consumed.
- How quickly the alcohol is consumed.
- A person's weight.
- A person's sex.
- Whether or not a person has eaten recently.

Ways to help prevent a guest from becoming intoxicated:

- Always check IDs.
- Do not serve the guest more than one drink at a time.
- Offer guest food when drinking.
- Keep track of how much a guest is consuming.

Know the stages of intoxication:

Level 1:
- Guest gets louder.
- Guest may become overly friendly.

Level 2:
- Guest may have difficulty walking.
- Speech may be slurred.
- Guest may become argumentative.
- Guest may have reduced muscle coordination (may have trouble picking up change, etc.).

How to Serve Alcohol

While you don't need to understand the distilling or fermenting processes, servers should be familiar with different types of alcohol, different glasses, and the basic terminology:

Serving

Waitstaff should always serve alcoholic beverages promptly. How quickly someone gets their drink can set the tone and mood for the customer that evening. If the server does not arrive with the drink for ten minutes, the customer realizes his or her meal service will probably be equally slow. If the server is backed up, a host or hostess or manager should step in and see that the table receives its drinks quickly. As with food, women are generally served first.

Glassware

Different glasses are used for different alcohol beverages. Make sure your servers know the difference between a jigger, highball glass, martini glass, and champagne flute, as well as the difference between red and white wine glasses. Make sure your servers always pick up glassware correctly. They should never touch the rim; glasses should be picked up by the handle or the base in the case of a wine glass.

Types of alcohol

In addition to knowing glassware, your server should be familiar with the different types of alcohol. For example, make sure your waitstaff knows that whiskey can refer to Irish whiskey, bourbon, rye, scotch, blended and Canadian.

Testing their knowledge

Test your servers' knowledge of alcohol and alcohol service. Make the test fun, however, by awarding a prize to the server who gets the highest score and the server who improved the most from the last test.

Types of Alcohol

All liquor served in the restaurant can be divided into two basic categories: *well* items and *call* items. Some restaurants establish a three-tier system: well, call, and premium liquor. Premium liqour would have an additional surcharge.

Well items are house liquors the restaurant serves. They are called well items because they are in a well speed rack in front of the bartender. Well liquors are used when a customer orders a particular drink without specifying a brand; i.e., a scotch and soda or a bourbon and water. For each major type of liquor such as bourbon, gin, vodka, scotch, tequila, rum, brandy and rye, you will need to select a well or house brand. The well liquor you select must be a popular and recognized brand which is moderately priced.

Call items are the more expensive, higher-quality types of liquor that a customer orders by the particular brand name: for example, a Cutty Sark scotch and soda or a Jack Daniel's bourbon and water. Call items are sometimes called back bar items because they are usually stored on the shelves behind the bar.

Whiskey

All whiskeys are distilled from fermented grains. Commonly used grains are barley, rye, corn and wheat. All whiskeys are aged in oak barrels. From this aging process they obtain their characteristic color, flavor and aroma.

Most whiskey consumed in this country is produced in either the United States, Canada, Scotland or Ireland. Each country produces its very own distinctive whiskeys. Whiskey can be divided into two basic types: straight whiskey and blended whiskey.

Straight whiskey is a whiskey that has never been mixed with other types of whiskey or with any neutral grain spirits. Straight whiskey itself has four major types, discussed below.

Blended whiskey is a blend of straight whiskeys and/or neutral grain spirits. It must contain at least 20 percent, by volume, of a straight whiskey and be bottled at no less than 80 proof.

Straight Whiskey

Bourbon whiskey. Its name is derived from Bourbon county in Kentucky, where the whiskey was originally produced. Bourbon must be distilled from grain mash containing at least 51 percent corn. (Suggested: 1 well bourbon and 3–6 call items.)

Rye whiskey. Rye has the similar amber color of bourbon, but the flavor and aroma are different. Rye whiskey must be distilled from a fermented mash of grain containing at least 51 percent rye. (Suggested: 1 well rye and 1–2 call items.)

Corn whiskey. Corn whiskey must be distilled from fermented mash of grain containing at least 80 percent corn. (Suggested: 1 call item only.)

Bottled in bond whiskey. Usually a rye or bourbon whiskey that is produced under the supervision of the U.S. government. The government ensures the following:

- The whiskey is aged at least four years.
- It is bottled at 100 proof.
- It is produced in one distilling by a single distiller.
- It is bottled and stored under government supervision.

Since the government bonds these steps, the whiskey referred to as "bottled in bond." The government does not guarantee the quality of the whiskey, it only ensures that these steps have been completed under its supervision. (Suggested: 1–2 call items.)

Blended Whiskeys

Canadian whiskey. Canadian whiskey is a blend produced under the supervision of the Canadian government. This whiskey is usually lighter-bodied than most American whiskeys. (Suggested: 1 well and 3–6 call items.)

Scotch whiskey. Scotch whiskey is produced only in Scotland. All Scotch blends contain malt and grain whiskeys. The unique smoky flavor of Scotch is derived from drying malted barley over open peat fires. In recent years the popularity of single malt scotch and other whiskey has grown phenomenally. Many bars have a vast selection of hard-to-find single malts, and they are very expensive and profitable. Single malt whisky is the product from a single distillery and has not been blended with any other whiskies. Only water is added before it is bottled, and in the case of "cask strength" bottlings, not even that. There are bottlings available with an alcohol-percentage of over 60! (Suggested: 1 well scotch and 4–8 call items.)

Irish whiskey. Irish whiskey is produced only in Ireland. This whiskey is usually heavier and fuller bodied than most Scotch blends. The malted barley used in the distilling process is dried over coal-fired kilns. This drying process has little or no affect on the whiskey's taste. (Suggested: 2–3 call items.)

Other Liquor

Vodka: Vodka was originally produced in Russia from distilled potatoes. Now, produced in various countries, vodka is commonly made from a variety of grains, the most common of which are wheat and corn. It is bottled at no less than 80 and no higher than 110 proof. During the distillation process, it is highly refined and filtered, usually through activated charcoal. Vodka is not aged. It is colorless, odorless and virtually tasteless. Because of these traits, it is a very versatile liquor that can be mixed with almost anything. In addition, it can be served straight, chilled to taste. (Suggested: 1 well brand at 80 proof and one at 110 proof, and 2–3 call items; 1–2 should be imported.)

Gin: Gin is distilled from a variety of grains and is bottled at 80 proof. Every gin manufactured has its own distinctive flavor and aroma. The aroma is derived from a recipe of juniper berries and other assorted plants. Gin is usually colorless and is most often used in making the popular martini cocktail. Vacuum-distilled gin is distilled in a glass-lined vacuum at lower than normal distilling temperature. This process tends to eliminate the bitterness found in some gins. (Suggested: 1 well and 3–4 call items; 1–2 should be imported.)

Rum: Rum is distilled from cane syrup, which is the fermented juice of sugar cane and molasses. It is bottled at no less than 80 proof. Most rums are a blend of many different types of aged rums. Dark rums often have caramel syrup added for color. Rums can be classified into two major types:

Light-bodied rums are dry and light in color due to a lack of molasses. Among the light-bodied rums are two varieties: gold label and white label. The gold is often of slightly better quality and is darker and sweeter; the white is paler and slightly stronger in flavor. (Suggested: 1 well 80 proof and 1–2 call items.)

Heavy-bodied rums have been distilled by a different and slower process. Because of the slowness of this process, the rum contains more molasses, which makes the rum darker, sweeter and richer. (Suggested: 1 well 80 proof, 2–3 call items and 1–2 high proof items.)

Brandy: Brandy is traditionally distilled from a mash of fermented grapes but may be produced from other fruits. There are many different types available.

Cognac: Cognac is perhaps the finest of distilled brandies. It is produced only in the Cognac region of France. Usually it is a blend of many different types of distilled cognac of the region. Cognac may be aged for as long as fifty years or more.

Armagnac brandy: This brandy is similar to cognac but slightly drier in taste. It is produced only in the Armagnac region of France.

Apple Jack: This brandy is distilled from the cider of crushed apples. Calvados (an apple brandy) is produced only in Normandy, France. In the United States, Apple Jack is often bottled in bond.

Fruit flavored brandies: These brandies have a distilled brandy base with a flavor ingredient added. These are commonly used in blended cocktails. A good selection of the more popular types will be needed.

Tequila: Tequila is usually produced in Mexico or the American southwest. It is distilled from the fermented mash of the aqua or century plants, which are cacti. Tequila is usually clear, although some types may have a gold tint. The smell and taste are distinctive. Tequila is used primarily in making margarita cocktails. Also in recent years there has been a wide increase in the variety of "premium" tequilas. Tequila can also be chilled and served straight as a "shooter" with a beer chaser. (Suggested: 1 well and 2–3 imported call items.)

Cordidals and Liqueurs: Cordials and liqueurs are created by the mixing or pre-distilling of neutral grain spirits with fruits, flowers or plants, to which sweeteners have been added. Cordials and liqueurs are all colorful and very sweet in taste, which is why they are usually served as after-dinner drinks. There are a wide variety of cordials and liqueurs available. A good selection of cordials and liqueurs would include 15 to 25 of these. There are approximately 10 to 12 different types that you must stock because of their popularity or because they are used in making certain cocktails. (All cordials and liqueurs should be call items.)

Vermouth: Vermouth is not classified as liqueur or liquor at all, but is actually a wine flavored with roots, berries or various types of plants. Vermouth is used almost exclusively in making martinis and manhattans. There are two basic types:

Dry vermouth is usually produced in America or France. This variety has a clear to light goldish color. It is used primarily in martini cocktails. One good well item is all that is required.

Sweet vermouth is a darker reddish wine with a richer, sweeter flavor. It is most often produced in Italy. Sweet vermouth is primarily used in making Manhattan cocktails. One good well item is all you'll need.

Beer

Whether packaged in bottles or kegs, beer should be treated as a food product. Always keep in mind that it is a perishable commodity with a limited life span. To ensure the freshness and full flavor of bottled beer, it's essential to adhere to a few simple procedures. The two biggest enemies of beer are exposure to light and temperature extremes, and the best way to combat them is to store beer in a dark, relatively cool place.

There are five basic categories for the hundreds of brands of beer produced. They are: **lagers**, the most popular type produced today; **ales**, which contain more hops and are stronger in flavor; and **porter**, **stout** and **bock** beers, which are all heavier, darker, richer and sweeter than the first two.

Beer is available in bottles, cans or on a draft keg system. Of the hundreds of brands available, fewer than a dozen are primarily demanded by customers. However, it should be noted that the popularity of "micro-brewed" beers has come on very strong. There are many independent restaurants and at least two national chains that use a micro-brewery in their own establishment as a marketing vehicle. It is suggested that your most popular beer be on draft — most customers prefer it that way, and it is cheaper for you. Beer is a perishable item, so you'll want to buy the other, less popular brands you'll carry in bottles or cans to preserve their freshness. Most draft systems can handle three separate kegs; if your business warrants it, use all of them. If your restaurant serves ethnic or international food, it's a nice touch to include some beer selections produced in that region or country.

Imported beers have gained increasing popularity in recent years. Although they are 50 to 100 percent more expensive than domestic beers, customers still demand the more popular ones. There are three to four of these imported beers that you should always stock.

Light beer is produced with fewer calories than other beer, and has developed a great demand within the past five years. One to two light beers should be included on your list.

 Fast Fact

Sixty-six percent of consumers say they eat a wider variety of ethnic foods than they did five years ago.[12]

12. The National Restaurant Organization, 2016

Bar Terms

Defined below are some common bar terms:

ALCOHOL. There are several types of alcohol. Ethyl alcohol is the type found in all alcoholic beverages.

PROOF. Proof is the measurement of alcohol in an alcoholic beverage. Each degree of proof represents a half percent of alcohol. For example, a bottle of liquor distilled at 90 proof is 45 percent alcohol.

GRAIN-NEUTRAL SPIRITS. This is a colorless, tasteless, usually odorless ethyl alcohol distilled from grain at a minimum of 190 proof. Grain-neutral spirits are used in blending whiskies and in making other types of liquor/liqueur.

SHOT or JIGGER. A shot or jigger is a unit of liquor ranging from ¾ ounce to 2 ounces. Most restaurants pour 1 ¼–1 ½-ounce shots for cocktails, and add slightly less to blended drinks.

STRAIGHT UP refers to a cocktail that is served with no ice — usually a martini, Manhattan or margarita. A special chilled, long-stem, straight-up glass should be used. Liqueurs and cordials that are served straight up may be poured into pony glasses.

ON THE ROCKS refers to a cocktail — usually a straight liquor, such as a scotch or a cordial — being served over ice. Although most cocktails are served over ice anyway, certain cocktails and liquors are just as commonly served without ice. In such cases the bartender or cocktail waitress must ask the customer which way she prefers.

TWIST, WEDGE and **SLICE** refer to the fruit that garnishes the cocktail glass. A twist is a lemon peel. A wedge or slice is usually a piece of lime or orange.

PRESS. Use a fruit press to squeeze the juice of a fruit garnish into the cocktail.

BITTERS is a commercially produced liquid made from roots, berries or a variety of herbs. It is, indeed, bitter, and a dash or two is used in some cocktails.

VIRGIN refers to a drink that contains no alcoholic beverage, such as a Virgin Piña-Colada or a Virgin Bloody Mary.

BACK. Usually refers to either a water or coffee back. This indicates that along with the cocktail ordered, the customer would also like a separate glass of water or cup of coffee.

RIMMED. Place either salt, sugar or celery salt around the rim of a cocktail glass. Usually Bloody Marys, Margaritas and Salty Dogs are served this way. The bartender prepares a rimmed glass by wetting the rim of the glass with a wedge of fruit, he then twirls the glass in a bowl of the salt or sugar desired.

SHAKEN refers to a cocktail that is shaken in the mixing glass before being strained.

STIRRED refers to a cocktail that is stirred (not shaken) in the mixing glass with a spoon before being strained.

Wine

Just a few years ago, many restaurants offered only two choices of wine: white or red. With the popularity of wine drinkers soaring, many restaurants now have extensive wine lists, ranging from the common to the rare. As wine's popularity continues to grow, on-premise consumption continues to expand beyond the traditional restaurants. Sales are being further increased by well-publicized and documented studies that indicate that wine can be good for one's health if consumed in moderation.

Serving wine in the restaurant may be as simplistic or as elaborate as you wish it to be. Some restaurants stock hundreds of bottles, many of rare vintages and kept in elaborate cellars. Others serve only a house wine or, even simpler, none at all. Wine, regardless of the vintage or cost, will always improve the customer's evening by enhancing the flavor of the entrées and making dinner a festive event. The purpose of this chapter is not to delve into the intricacies of wine, but to demonstrate how to develop and promote a sensible wine list. By developing such a wine list, you will not only increase your customers' enjoyment of wine, but will increase the restaurant's profits as well. Developing the wine list is just the start, however, of a wine program; server training is imperative. Wine education is way down on the list of things that the restaurateur has the time to think about; however, wine is one of the items that could impact the restaurateur's bottom line the most significantly.

While wine is alcohol, we treat it separately here because there are more nuances to wine service than the service of other alcoholic beverages. Many people enjoy drinking wine with food, so the service of wine involves a greater knowledge of the wine itself than with other alcoholic drinks. If someone orders a scotch and soda for dinner, they don't worry whether it goes with the lamb special. When a guest orders wine, however, they usually try to pair it with the food they are ordering. Because of the important link between food and wine, many restaurants do not take a wine order until after the guests have placed their food orders. The following guidelines will help you serve wine with flair.

Bottle Sizes

Most restaurants have 750-milliliter wine bottles for bottle sales. They may also offer splits of wine or champagne, which are generally half the size of a regular bottle. Most restaurants also stock larger bottles of house wines to use for individual glass service.

Wine Language

It is important that your servers know the basics about wine, the most common grape varieties, and how people discuss wine. Your servers should be able to discuss wines' color and smell ("nose") and taste ("palate"). You may also want them to be able to distinguish more subtle color difference. Is the wine yellow like a Chardonnay or is it clearer like a Pinot Grigio? Some of the terms people use to describe smell and taste include dry, sweet, earthy and smoky. They may also say that a wine's taste is reminiscent of another flavor, such as raspberries or pepper. Most importantly, your servers should know which wines in your establishment are sweet and which are dry. This will be the main category upon which guests will base their wine decisions. For helpful advice about wine language, as well as information on reading wine labels, visit: **www.winefolly.com**.

Helping a Customer Choose Wine

Many customers will look to the server for expert advice on what wine to choose. Make sure your servers are comfortable in this role. To do this, the first thing that must happen is that the servers need to be familiar with the restaurant's wine list and how all the wines taste. If the customer is particularly wine savvy, the server could suggest getting a manager or someone else with greater wine knowledge to help the customer. You should also encourage servers to let customers have a taste of the wines that you offer by the glass.

 Fast Fact

Thirty-nine percent of consumers say they would pay their bar tab through a smartphone app if offered.[13]

13. The National Restaurant Organization, 2016

Serving Wine

Red wines should be served at room temperature, and white wines should be chilled to about 50 degrees. To serve a bottle of wine, present the bottle to the person that ordered it, with the label facing the customer. Once the customer has approved the wine, set the bottle on the corner of the table to open it. Cut the foil off the lower lip of the bottle top and put the foil in your apron pocket. Remove the cork and pour an ounce or two for the person who ordered it to taste. You can also set the cork beside this person so they can inspect it, if they choose. After the customer has tasted and approved the wine, pour the wine for all the guests partaking, starting with the women in the group. When you finish pouring a glass, give the bottle a half turn as you raise it to help keep from making spills. Also keep a napkin next to the bottleneck to catch any spills. When filling wine glasses, the server should fill to one-half or two-thirds.

Pronunciation

Be sure your servers are familiar with how to pronounce all the wines on your wine list.

Wine and Food

Your servers should know how to suggest what wine will complement what entrée. You can help them out by including this information on your menu if there is room, but servers still need to know how to make suggestions for your customers.

Wine Resources

There are many books and magazines about wine. Some of the more respectable publications include *Exploring Wine: The Culinary Institute of America's Complete Guide to Wines of the World*, Robert Parker's *Buying Guide*, Oz Clarke's *Encyclopedia of Wine*, Hugh Johnson's *Wine Atlas*, and Tom Steven's *New Sotheby's Wine Encyclopedia*.

Hachette Wine Guide

Recognized as *The French Wine Bible* and *The Definitive Guide to French Wine*, the Hachette Wine Guide contains over 9,000 wines chosen and described by 900 experts.

Online

Try Wine Spectator at **www.winespectator.com**, Wine and Spirits at **www.wineandspiritsmagazine.com**, and Wine Enthusiast at **www .wineenthusiast.com**. There also are web resources for information on wine. Tasting Wine (**www.tasting-wine.com**) is a good resource, as is WineMag's wine terminology web page at **www.winemag.com/glossary**. Finally, the American Institute of Wine and Food's website has information on local chapters at **www.aiwf.org**, and Wines.com at **www.wines .com** offers expert answers, virtual wine tastings and an online searchable database.

Wine Labels

In the United States, wine labels have the following information:

- Name of wine
- Name of producer\name and address of bottler
- Name of importer
- Name of shipper
- Alcohol content (as a percentage of volume)
- Country of origin
- Sulfite advisory
- Government warning

Labels may also include:

- Quality of wine
- Vintage
- Type of wine
- Growing region
- Descriptive information

Wine labeling regulations are determined by the regulatory body in each country, so wines from areas other than the United States may contain different information on their labels.

The following descriptions are the basic classifications of wine, what menu items are best served with them, and the approximate number to stock in order to represent each category adequately.

REDS

Light-bodied (Gamay, Sangiovese, Pinot Noir) — red meats, roasted poultry, and oily fish such as salmon

Medium-bodied (Merlot, Syrah, Zinfandel, Malbec) — veal, pork, venison, game birds

Full-bodied (Cabernet Sauvignon) — all red meats, duck, lamb

Semi-sweet — dessert; never before dinner, as the sweetness will spoil the customer's appetite

WHITES

Dry light-bodied (Pinot Grigio, Pinot Blanc, some Rieslings) — shellfish, some seafood

Semi-sweet — seafood

Medium-bodied (Sauvignon Blanc, Gewürztraminer, some Chardonnays) — roasted poultry, oily fish such as salmon, steak

Full-bodied (Chardonnay) — white meats, seafood

ROSÉ

Dry light-bodied — can be served in place of either dry white or red wines

SPARKLING WINE/CHAMPAGNE

Dry — May be served in place of dry white wines — compliments most foods.

Semi-sweet — May be served in place of semi-sweet whites — does not go with as much as a dry sparkling wine.

FORTIFIED AND DESSERT WINES

Sherry — soup course.

Sweeter wines go well with fruit and/or dessert.

Some, such as Port or Sauterne can go with a savory appetizer such as Stilton cheese.

Tasting Tips

Seeing

You can tell several things from the color of a wine, including its age; white wines grow darker with age, and red wines grow lighter.

Swirling

Smell is an important part of wine tasting. In order to smell all the nuances in a wine, you want to swirl the wine in your glass to "open it up." Swirling allows air to combine with the wine. To swirl, hold the glass by its stem and rotate in a small circle.

Smelling

After swirling the wine, smell it and try to describe the aroma.

Sipping

When tasting wine, you should take small amounts into your mouth and hold them at the bottom of your mouth. Draw in air through a small hole in your lips and let the air cross the wine in your mouth, allowing it to bubble.

Describing Wine

Light: Refers to the wine's body and/or alcohol content.

Dry: Refers to the lack of sweetness in the wine.

Semi-Sweet: Refers to the underlying sweetness of a wine.

Body: The texture or taste of the wine in the mouth.

Bouquet: Many aromas are found in a single wine.

Buttery: Rich, creamy aroma and flavor. Usually used to describe some Chardonnays.

Finish: The flavor a wine leaves in the mouth after the wine is swallowed.

Legs: The drops of wine that run down the inside of the glass when it is swirled.

Mature: Ready to drink.

Nose: The aroma or bouquet of a wine.

Bright: A young wine with fresh, fruity flavors.

Chewy: Heavy, tannic, full-bodied wines.

Crisp: A noticeably acidic wine, but the acid does not overpower the wine.

Dense: A full-flavored wine or wine with a deep color.

Earthy: Can be a positive or negative characteristic. It may refer to a pleasant, clean quality or a funky, dirty character.

Fat: A full-bodied, high-alcohol wine.

Forward: An early maturing wine.

Fragrant: A wine with a floral aroma or bouquet.

Jammy: A sweet, concentrated fruit flavor.

Peppery: A wine with a spicy, black pepper flavor.

Robust: Full-flavored, intense wine.

Round: A wine with a well-balanced, mellow and full-bodied flavor.

Soft: A wine that is mellow and well balanced.

Aggressive: The wine has slightly high tannins or acid.

Flat: A wine that lacks flavor due to the lack of acidity in it.

Metallic: A wine with a tin-like flavor.

Off: A wine that is flawed or spoiled.

Sharp: A wine with too much acid.

Glassware

Choosing the wine glass is an important consideration. The wine glass you use will have an apparent effect upon the taste of the wine. Should you doubt this, compare the same wine in a fine crystal glass and then again in a cheap glass; you should notice a difference. This is not to say you should use crystal wine glasses, but purchase the best ones affordable.

Many restaurants use a separate glass for reds, whites and champagnes. This is generally unnecessary. A 10-ounce tulip-shaped glass would be quite suitable for any wine. However, it is a nice touch to have separate champagne glasses.

Serving Wine

Wine is a delicate substance. It must be cared for and served properly in order for it to taste the way it should. Each delivery must be properly received and stored away from light, heat sources and vibrations. Wine must be stored on its side or at enough of an angle to keep the cork moist. Should the bottle be stored upright the cork will soon dry out and allow air to seep into the bottle and spoil the taste of the wine.

The most important consideration in serving wine is to make certain it is at the proper temperature. Much of the wine's flavor, bouquet and body will be lost if it is served too cold or too warm. Most people know that red wines should be served at room temperature, but this is a confusing statement. "Room temperature" in Europe is 10 to 15 degrees cooler than in North America. For clarification, the list below gives the commonly accepted serving temperatures for each wine. However, these are not steadfast rules, as taste is an individual experience, and individuals have different preferences. Always serve wine in the manner the customer wishes.

White and Rosé: 46–50 degrees Fahrenheit

Red Wines: 62–68 degrees Fahrenheit

Champagne and Sparkling: 42–48 degrees Fahrenheit

(Serve in an ice bucket with water.)

Always ask the customer when he or she would like the wine to be served or with which course. Red wines should be opened as soon as possible and placed on the table so that they may "breathe." This allows air to enter the bottle, which is supposed to release the wine's flavor and bouquet. Many experts will argue that this step is unnecessary because of the minimal amount of air actually exposed to the wine at the neck of the bottle. Whether or not it is effective, it should always be done for appearance's sake. White wines and champagnes may need to be cooled prior to serving, so take the wine order as soon as possible.

Steps for proper wine service:

1. Always place a napkin behind the bottle.

2. Display the bottle to the person who ordered it (usually the host). Give him plenty of time to examine the label: he will want to make sure it is the wine and vintage desired.

3. The wine opener used should be the waitperson's folding pocket-knife with the open spiral corkscrew and smooth edges.

4. With the knife blade, remove the capsule and foil.

5. Clean the neck and bottle with the napkin.

6. Hold the bottle firmly, and slowly insert the corkscrew into the center of the cork. Stop about two-thirds of the way through the cork. Don't go all the way, as this may result in putting a few pieces of the cork into the wine.

7. With the bottle on the table, pull straight up steadily; do not jerk out the cork.

8. After opening, check the cork for dryness, and place it end up on the table so that the host may examine it.

9. When the host is satisfied, pour about an ounce into his glass. He must approve of the wine before the other people in the party are served.

10. The customer has the prerogative to reject a bottle of wine at any stage of the service. However, once the bottle is opened, his reasoning for rejection must be due to there being something wrong with the wine itself, not because he doesn't like it. If a bottle is rejected, it should be removed from the table and brought to the kitchen where the manager may examine it and act accordingly. Some distributors may issue a credit for damaged bottles, however there is usually no obligation to do so, particularly with older, more expensive bottles.

11. It is customary to pour all the women's glasses first and the host's last. When you are finished pouring a glass, give the bottle a slight twist: this will prevent any dripping. Always pour wine with the label facing you.

Opening sparkling wine and champagne:

1. Always use a napkin behind the bottle to stop drips, and although it rarely happens, it is possible that the bottle may split from the internal pressure.

2. Remove the foil and wire muzzle.

3. Remove the cork by turning the bottle, not the cork. Always point the bottle away from people. The cork should be removed slowly and carefully, it should never explode open with a gush of champagne.

4. Special champagne glasses may be used, however it is perfectly acceptable to serve champagne in tulip-shaped wine glasses.

5. A stuck cork may be removed by placing the neck of the bottle under a stream of hot water for a few seconds. The heat will build up pressure on the inside of the bottle making it easier to extract the cork.

Pouring Procedures

Liquor, as all food items, must be portioned in order to control costs and maintain consistency in the final product. The following training outline and suggestions will help you to maintain beverage-portion consisteny with your serving and bar staff.

Liquor is portioned not by weight but by volume. Volume is measured in shots or jiggers, which are liquid measurements ranging from ¾ ounce to

2 ounces. Most restaurants pour between 1 ¼ and 1 ½ ounces per cocktail and slightly less — 1⅛ to 1¼ ounces — for blended drinks.

The first step in developing consistent pouring procedures is to determine the amount of liquor each drink will contain. It is suggested that you use the amount stated above for each shot. More than 1½ ounce of liquor in a cocktail will make it too strong and dominate the liquor's flavor, which many people do not care for. A cocktail containing less than 1⅛ ounces of liquor will be too weak and may give customers the impression that you are trying to cut corners.

There are two basic ways to portion-control liquor: a computerized bar gun and a free-pouring bartender. Both systems have advantages and disadvantages.

A computerized bar gun is by far the best way to control and account for every shot of liquor poured. Although there are many different types and models available, all basically operate the same. Each well item is hooked up to a hose that runs to the bar. The well items are hidden either underneath the bar or behind the back wall in an adjacent room. The hose at the bar is hooked into a gun which is similar to the one used for the soda canisters. Small buttons on the face of the gun indicate each of the well items. When the bartender presses a button, the exact measurement of liquor is dispensed. The number and type of liquor poured is automatically recorded and written up with the correct price. A tape is simultaneously run showing the updated number and type of cocktails poured over the night. As previously stated, there are many variations on this system, but they can all determine if there has been any loss of liquor or revenue.

✕ Fast Fact

There are liquor pour spouts available that are simply placed on the bottle and dispense only one shot at a time. These are effective, and by simply turning the bottle upright again, the bartender can dispense another shot.

There are two distinct disadvantages to the computerized bar gun. The first and foremost: the bar tends to loose its aesthetic value. Computerized bars may be applauded by accountants and restaurant owners, but they are generally frowned upon by the public. The restaurant and lounge should be a place where a person can go to get away from the hustle and bustle of the modern world. He or she should be able to get a cocktail made by a professional and enjoy it with companions in a warm atmosphere and comfortable environment. The last thing most customers wish to see is some unknown liquor dribble out of a hose into a glass while a set of digital lights flash across the register. The art and showmanship of mixology is an important part of the environment and the atmosphere of a restaurant. A computerized bar may eliminate this integral part of the dining experience.

The second disadvantage to the computerized bar is the substantial investment needed to purchase one. Although it may pay for itself over a period of time, it is still an expensive start-up cost. Perhaps this is the reason bar guns are not, as of yet, universally used throughout the food service industry.

These two disadvantages of the computerized bar are the primary advantages of the free-pour system. The cost of operation is negligible: a few shot glasses and a pouring spout for each bottle is all that is required. The aesthetic value gained is immeasurable. It is impossible to put a value on atmosphere and taste. A good compromise is the use of the pour spouts that dispense an exact portion.

The main disadvantage to the free-pour system is, of course, the lack of control over and accountability for each shot poured. However, if bartenders are properly trained and supervised in the procedures described, there will be little problem in controlling the cost and consistency of the product. Bartenders, as all other employees in the restaurant, may become lax in using all the procedures in which they were trained. This is why, if a consistent, profitable operation is to be maintained, management must follow up, note and review all procedures with each and every employee.

Free-Pouring

There are two basic methods for free-pouring liquor. The first method is used primarily by beginners and inexperienced free-pour bartenders. This technique uses a fluted shot glass with a line drawn across the top of the glass at the level of the shot desired. The bartender simply places the shot glass on the bar or spill mat and pours until the liquid reaches the line. Then he or she pours the contents of the shot glass into the cocktail glass over the ice. This method is very accurate, but it is much slower and far less aestheticly pleasing than the second.

The second technique requires several weeks of full-time practice to master. Use an empty liquor bottle filled with water to practice pouring. This method gives the customer the impression that you have filled the shot glass once and then, after you have emptied the shot, continued to pour more liquor into the cocktail. In fact, what you did was measure out approximately ¾ of an ounce into the shot glass, emptied it into the cocktail, then made up the difference by pouring directly from the bottle into the drink, measuring by silently counting off, until you have reached the full shot.

To pour:

1. Grasp the bottle around the neck with your right hand (reverse if left-handed). Place your index finger around the pour spout.

2. Hold the ¾-ounce shot glass in your left hand above the cocktail glass and place the pour spout into the shot glass. Begin to pour. As you are pouring, angle the shot glass downward. When it nears capacity, spill the contents into the cocktail glass. Continue to point the pour spout into the glass while pouring. At this point you will have poured slightly less than ¾ of an ounce.

3. The difference will now be made up by pouring directly into the cocktail glass from the bottle. In order to measure exactly the amount to pour into the cocktail glass directly, count to yourself while pouring. To determine the correct count for the remaining ½ to ¾ ounce, experiment by counting while pouring into a lined shot glass.

Bartenders should be tested periodically to ensure they are pouring the required number of shots from each bottle. This is the figure that directly determines the price of each drink. To compute the number of shots you *should* get from each bottle, divide the bottle volume in ounces by the size of the average shot poured. Bottle spouts are available in a variety of speeds: fast, medium and slow; there's also a wide-mouthed juice spout. The speed at which the liquor flows is determined by the size of the air hole in the spout stopper. Partially covering this hole while pouring will regulate the flow. Fast-pour spouts should be used on liquors that are thick and syrupy, such as cordials. Medium pourers should be used on most bottles. Slow spouts may be used on any liquor that is poured in a shot containing less than 1⅛ ounces. Some expensive brandies and cordials are often poured at only 1 ounce. A slow pourer will give the effect of a long pour.

Some hints on bar organization:

- Set up glasses and ice first.
- Make blended drinks next.

- Once you pick up the shot glass, don't put it down until everything is poured.

- Once you pick up a bottle, pour into all the glasses needed.

- Allow at least ¼ inch of space at the top of each cocktail to allow for garnishes, straws, etc.

Pouring Draft Beer

Draft beer should be poured so that it produces a head that rises just above the top of the glass or pitcher. This will settle down to about three-fourths of an inch in a few minutes. This head or foam has both great economical and aesthetic value.

The size of the head is controlled by the angle of the glass or mug to the spout when you begin to pour. Should the head be too small, you will be pouring more beer into each glass; this will lead to a lower than expected yield on each keg. Since the customer is swallowing the CO_2 gas that would normally escape from the head, she will probably drink less head that is too large may give the customer the impression that you are attempting to cut corners on quality.

The most important consideration in serving beer is to use cold, spotless glasses or mugs. Glasses that appear clean may have a residual buildup of soap or grease. The slightest trace of these agents will break down the head and bubbles in the beer leaving a stale-looking product. Every glass used should be rinsed with cold, fresh water before filling. Always use a new glass for each beer ordered.

The temperature at which beer is served is also a crucial element. To ensure that the proper flavor is released, all beer should be served at 40 degrees Fahreheit. When beer is served below 38 degrees Fahrenheit it looses its distinct taste and aroma. Beer served above 42 degrees Fahreheit may turn cloudy and will loose its zest and flavor. Draft beer is not pasteurized, so it must always be held at a constant temperature. All beer coolers should be set at 38 degrees Fahrenheit so that the proper serving temperature can be maintained. Remember to always use chilled glasses and mugs (with thick glass and handles) to help keep the beer at a cool, constant temperature.

✕ Fast Fact

Beer lines must be flushed out weekly, just like soda lines. Beer is only as good as the lines through which it flows. The service of a professional tap and line cleaner are needed weekly. Your beer distributor can recommend a reputable company.

Pouring a perfect draft

Pouring a perfect beer with every pull of the tap handle takes some skill, but it can be easily mastered with practice. The procedures listed below offer some tips for maximizing draft beer service.

- Start with a "beer clean" glass.

- The size of the head is determined by the angle at which the glass is held under the spout at the start of the draw (never let the glass come in direct contact with the spout itself). If the glass is held at a sharp angle so that the beer flows down the side of the glass, there will be little or no head. Conversely, if the glass is held straight so that the beer splashes directly into the bottom of the glass, there will be a large head.

- For flat-bottomed glassware (such as an hourglass): Open the tap all the way by grasping the handle at its base and pulling it quickly (grasping at the top of the tap handle will result in too slow an open and the beer will come out overly foamy). Tilt the glass at about a 45-degree angle at the beginning of the pour and then straighten it up so that the beer splashes directly into the glass. The resulting head should be about ½ to 1 inch thick.

- For wide-bottomed glassware (such as a schooner or goblet): Don't tilt the glass at all. Open the tap as indicated above and allow the beer to pour directly into the bottom of the glass. The result should be a ½- to 1-inch head.

🍴 Fast Fact

Unchilled glassware will have a warming effect on beer. A thin, room-temperature glass will increase the temperature of the beer about 2 degrees Fahrenheit. An unchilled mug will raise the temperature of the beer about 4 to 6 degrees Fahrenheit.

Common Beer-Pouring Problems

Flat Beer

- Glasses are not "beer clean"
- Not enough CO_2 pressure
- Pressure shut off at closing
- Cooler or dispensing system too cold
- Leak in pressure tubing or barrels
- Loose tap or pressure connections
- Defective pressure-check valve in tap
- Sluggish pressure regulator
- Obstruction in line near barrel
- Compressor too small or inefficient
- Oily air from compressor or kitchen
- Long exposure to air instead of CO_2 gas pressure

Loose foam (settles quickly)

- Pressure required does not correspond to beer temperature (system is not balanced)

- Beer line system/coils not as cold as beer in barrel

- Beer dispensed through small diameter tubing into large shanks and faucets

Unpalatable beer

- Dirty faucets

- Dirty beer system

- Coils not cleaned properly

- Failure to flush beer lines with water after each empty barrel

- Failure to leave water in beer lines overnight

- Unsanitary conditions at bar

- Foul air or dirt in lines or air tank

- Oily air from kitchen

- Improper location, maintenance and lubrication of air pump

- Failure to provide fresh air inlet for air pump

- Failure to purge condensation from compressor storage tank

- Temperature of beer in barrel too warm

- Dry glasses

Sour beer

If the problem is sour beer, the difficulty is due to the temperature of the keg itself, either in the restaurant or bar, at the distributor's warehouse or en route. The beer should always be maintained at between 36 and 38 degrees Fahrenheit under normal operation. It should never be allowed to warm to 50 degrees Fahrenheit or more for any length of time, since this may begin a secondary fermentation.

Real Whipped Cream

All coffee drinks and many blended drinks use whipped cream as a topping or garnish. Real whipped cream is simple and inexpensive to prepare. The alternative to real whipped cream is the widely used aerosol can of (usually non-dairy) whipped cream. Real whipped cream is superior to the canned variety. The taste, texture and quality of the ingredients are incomparable.

Though there are many recipes, real whipped cream is made primarily with sugar, vanilla and heavy or whipping cream. Real whipped cream is often used in the kitchen for topping desserts and other items. To prepare, whip these ingredients in a mixing bowl for several minutes. Care must be taken not to overwhip.

✖ *Fast Fact*

Real whipped cream can be made by whipping the ingredients in the blender at the bar.

Freshly Squeezed Juices

A most impressive demonstration of quality is the use of freshly squeezed juices. Throughout the evening, the bartender can extract fresh juice for cocktails that use the juice of oranges, grapefruits, lemons and limes. The additional cost of using fresh juices is passed on to the customer through higher drink prices.

Any of the major food service distributors can supply a juice extractor. Advise your produce supplier of your intentions; make certain he or she can furnish the restaurant with fresh fruit year-round at an affordable price. The produce supplier should be able to get a discount on bruised or damaged fruit that, because of its appearance, cannot be sold as A-1 eating grade but may be used for juicing.

Garnishes

Garnishes sell drinks. Garnishes are part of the entertainment of drinking. There is nothing worse than a customer seeing less than fresh garnishes laying in a tray from the previous night that are about to go into his or her drink. They look bad and cost operators money in waste. Calculate how much is needed and cut just enough.

Heads turn when customers glimpse a pair of sunglasses or plastic animals hanging off a cocktail. Try using dry ice; a triple garnish of orange, lime and lemon slices; a cluster of grapes for the glass of wine; a choice of olives, such as almond- or garlic-stuffed olives; a lemon twist wrapped around a coffee bean; a skewer of oversized cherries; or a pickled okra sprout.

🍴 *Fast Fact*

Garnishes add finesse and style and can become a customer favorite or even a trademark of your restaurant's bar.

Be creative when adding a drink's garnish. Review some food-garnishing books and let your inventive chef have a crack at some ideas.

Enhancing Drink Quality

Sometimes the only element which separates successful restaurants from those that fail is in the small professional touches of excellence. This extra effort implies that a tremendous effort has been made all around to attain the highest level of quality possible. These subtle signs of concern are most important in the bar and lounge area, where the product is prepared and served in the open under the watchful and interested eyes of the customers. Professional bartenders and courteous cocktail waitresses can be found in any well-managed restaurant. However, it is the small, undemanded touches and extra procedures that separate good lounges from superb ones. Described in this section are some simple, inexpensive suggestions which will give your bar and lounge the extra touches — the finesse — that will separate yours from the rest.

Heated snifters

Snifter glasses should always be warmed prior to pouring brandy and certain cordials. Brandy heated in a warm glass has a stronger aroma and flavor that is preferred by most people.

To heat the brandy snifter, pour near-boiling water into the bottom third of the glass. Let it sit for two to three minutes. Before using, wipe the entire glass dry with a clean bar towel. Coffee-drink glasses and mugs should also be preheated as described to maintain the coffee's temperature. You may also preheat glasses by filling them with tap water and microwaving them for 15–30 seconds.

Frosted beer mugs

Beer mugs and glasses should be frosted prior to use. Aside from adding aesthetic value to the beer, chilled glasses help maintain it at the proper drinking temperature.

Stock a supply of the mugs in a cooler set at 31–33 degrees Fahrenheit. When the mugs are removed from the cooler, condensation will occur, leaving the frosted glass with a thin layer of ice. Mugs must be dry when placed in the cooler. Should they contain droplets from a recent washing, this excess water will freeze onto the mug. When defrosted by the warmth of the beer, this ice will melt, diluting the beer, and depriving the customer of its delicate flavor.

Chilled cocktail straight-up glasses

Chilled cocktail straight-up glasses must be kept ice cold, as the cocktails themselves contain no ice. These glasses are used almost exclusively for straight-up martinis, Manhattans, gibsons and margaritas. If there is no cooler space available to keep a supply chilled, bury them stem-up in crushed ice. Glasses must be shaken dry before using.

Flaming liquor

Certain cocktails require that they be set aflame prior to serving. Extreme care must be used by employees and customers when handling these cocktails. Preheat the glass and warm the entire cocktail before attempting to ignite it. Remove a teaspoon of the cocktail and set it aflame. Pour the flaming liquid carefully back into the cocktail.

 **Fast Fact**

Fire regulations in your area may prohibit any open flames, such as those from candles, flaming food, and flaming liquor. Contact the local fire department to learn of its restrictions.

Fresh fruit daiquiries

Fresh fruit daiquiries are incomparable in quality to daiquiries which are made from fruit-flavored liqueurs. Unfortunately, most bars prepare the latter. Aside from being a misrepresentation, substituting fruit-flavored liqueurs for real fruit is unnecessary. Fresh fruit is available in most places year-round. The small additional cost and bother is outweighed by the resulting quality of the cocktail.

Glassware is an important consideration when promoting specialty drinks. The proper glass for each cocktail is essential. The appearance and the presentation are almost as important as the drink's taste. As a final touch, use a piece of freshly cut fruit to garnish the rim.

Fresh fruit daiquiries and other specialty drinks should be promoted; these cocktails are very popular and profitable items. Be creative: develop some house specialties and give them exotic names. Employees must become enthusiastic about a promotion in order for it to become a success. Encourage them through monetary incentives to sell. Let them try the different specialty drinks; if they enjoy them, they will promote them with vigor. Point out that the larger the average check, the larger the tip the employee will receive.

Floating cordials – pousse cafe

The most attractive cordial served uses a variety of liqueurs which are floating in layers, one on top of the other in the same glass. This presentation amazes customers and will bring praise to the bartender and restaurant. Although it appears complicated — if not impossible — to create, the floating cordial is actually rather simple. Liqueurs and cordials have different densities, thus enabling liqueurs with lower densities to float atop those with higher densities. The trick is to pour the liqueur carefully on top of the preceding one. This can be best accomplished by pouring each liqueur over an inverted spoon. The rounded bottom of the spoon will diffuse the liquid over the one below and no mixing will occur. Be certain that all ingredients given in the recipe are poured in the exact order listed.

Creating the peacock effect with napkins

Undoubtedly you have seen in fancy bars the stacks of cocktail napkins displayed like the feathers of a peacock, all jutting out in a different circular direction. Although this appears to be a painstakingly difficult and time-consuming task, in actuality it is easily and quickly created. The bartender can prepare an entire night's napkins in less than five minutes.

Place a two-inch-high stack of cocktail napkins on the bar. Place a small highball glass on its side in the middle of the stack. Press down on the glass and rotate it two to three inches to the left. Move the glass around to each side until the napkins are all feathered out evenly. This is an extremely simple procedure which results in elegant-looking napkins.

Chapter 14

Bussing

Although the bus person has one of the least glamorous of the restaurant jobs, it is still one of the most important. Bussers have many different tasks and help a variety of different employees, but their primary job is to keep things clean and organized. Ever gone to an eating joint with bad restrooms, messy tables, or crumbs all over the floor? Not very appetizing. No matter how good the food is or how snappy the service, a bus person can make all the difference between a customer having a good or bad experience at your restaurant.

The following table outlines the bus person's job responsibilities.

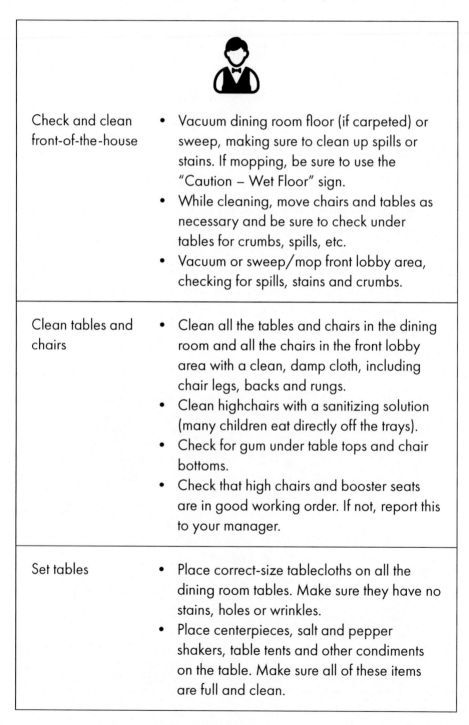

Check and clean front-of-the-house	• Vacuum dining room floor (if carpeted) or sweep, making sure to clean up spills or stains. If mopping, be sure to use the "Caution – Wet Floor" sign. • While cleaning, move chairs and tables as necessary and be sure to check under tables for crumbs, spills, etc. • Vacuum or sweep/mop front lobby area, checking for spills, stains and crumbs.
Clean tables and chairs	• Clean all the tables and chairs in the dining room and all the chairs in the front lobby area with a clean, damp cloth, including chair legs, backs and rungs. • Clean highchairs with a sanitizing solution (many children eat directly off the trays). • Check for gum under table tops and chair bottoms. • Check that high chairs and booster seats are in good working order. If not, report this to your manager.
Set tables	• Place correct-size tablecloths on all the dining room tables. Make sure they have no stains, holes or wrinkles. • Place centerpieces, salt and pepper shakers, table tents and other condiments on the table. Make sure all of these items are full and clean.

	• Place the correct number of silverware sets and glasses on all tables. Do not use any glassware or silverware that is dirty or chipped.
Clearing and resetting tables	• Gather the items you will need for resetting tables throughout the night (bus pans, clean silver, clean glasses, new condiments, etc.). • Clean tables and reset within 5 minutes of the guests' departure. This should be done as quietly as possible so as not to disturb other guests. • Scrap food debris into bus pan. This should be done out of view of other customers. If you can't do it out of view in the dining room, wait until you go into the back kitchen. • Put dirty dishes, silver and glassware in the bus pan, carefully stacking like items so nothing breaks. • Clean the table either by wiping it with a sanitized rag if there is no tablecloth or by replacing the tablecloth, if necessary. • Clean condiment containers and table tents. • Reset the table, making sure all new items are clean and free of chips or cracks. • Clean chairs and check floor under table, use a push broom if there are crumbs underneath the table.

Chapter 15
Sanitation and Safety

Sure, your restaurant is a well-oiled machine, but it's still a building full of humans. No matter how well you've trained your staff, an employee could still cut himself on a meat slicer, or a customer could choke on a cherry tomato. Humans make mistakes, and workplace accidents happen—it's how you respond to them that makes all the difference between life and death. The first thing to do is to have a safety plan in place and train your servers to know and understand the elements of this plan so that they can respond calmly and quickly. For another layer of safety, you could also ask an outside agency such as the American Red Cross or your local fire department come in for safety training.

Red Cross

The Red Cross can make sure all of your servers know universal precautions, first aid, the abdominal thrust maneuver and CPR. You can contact the Red Cross at **www.redcross.org**.

Fire department

Your local fire department will give your employees free training on how to use fire extinguishers. More fires occur in food service than in any other type of operation. Fire extinguishers should be available in all areas where fires are likely, especially in the kitchen near grills and deep fryers. But be careful—don't keep extinguishers so close to the equipment that they will be inaccessible in the event of a fire. All employees should be trained in avoiding fires as well as in the use of fire extinguishers and in evacuation procedures. Remember, always call the fire department first, before using a fire extinguisher!

OSHA

The Occupational Safety and Health Agency (OSHA) is the federal agency that oversees safety in the workplace. It can also provide you with safety-training information. Make sure you are in compliance with all their regulations. To find out more about their requirements for food service establishments and to explore training materials they offer, visit them on line at **www.osha.gov**.

Preventing Accidents

Accidents are both dangerous and costly. Most accidents are avoidable and are the results of such careless acts as:

- Failure to immediately clean up foods spilled on the floor to prevent anyone slipping.

- Failure to set trays and dishes back from the edges of the side tables or counters so that they will not be knocked off in passing.

- Loading trays in such a way that the dishes will slide off.

- Piling dishes in tall stacks that may tip easily.

- Failure to nest cups by turning the handles in opposite directions to make them fit together securely.

- Stacking piles of dishes unevenly so that the stack is likely to tip.

- Carrying several water glasses in the fingers so that the rims touch (they frequently are cracked or nicked by this method of handling).

- Failure to keep long handles on containers turned away from the edges of the hot plates or counters.

- Leaving cupboard doors ajar so that a person may hit the corner and be injured.

- Failure to enter the serving pantry and kitchen by the entrance door ("In") and to leave by the exit door ("Out"). (If there is only one door, open it carefully to avoid hitting someone who may be entering from the other side.)

- Not watching the movement of other employees in the vicinity, and moving immediately into their paths without warning them.

- Not warning the guests when plates, containers or handles are very hot.

- Failure to hold hot plates and handles with the side towel to avoid burns.

Strains

Carrying equipment or food items that are too heavy can result in strains to the arms, legs, or back. A strain is an injury generally caused by overexertion or misuse of a muscle.

To prevent strains:

- Store heavy items on lower shelves.

- Use dollies or carts when moving objects that are too heavy to carry.

- Use carts with firm shelves and properly operating wheels or casters to move objects from one area to another.

- Don't carry too many objects at one time; instead, use a cart.

- Don't try to lift large or heavy objects by yourself.

- Use proper lifting techniques; remember to bend from your knees, not your back.

Slipping and Falling

Anyone who slips and falls onto the floor can be badly hurt. Be sure your facility does not have hazards that put workers and customers at risk.

To prevent slips and falls:

- Clean up wet spots and spills immediately.

- Let people know when floors are wet. Use signs that signal caution, and prominently display them. Wear shoes that have no-slip soles.

- Do not stack boxes or other objects too high; they can fall and cause people to trip.

- Keep items such as boxes, ladders, step stools and carts out of the paths of foot traffic.

Fires

Fire extinguishers should be available in all areas where fires are likely, especially in the kitchen near grills and deep fryers. But be careful: don't keep extinguishers so close to the equipment that they will be inaccessible in the event of a fire.

🍴 Fast Fact

More fires occur in food service than in any other type of operation.

All employees should be trained in avoiding fires as well as in the use of fire extinguishers and in evacuation procedures. Remember: always call the fire department first, before using a fire extinguisher!

Choking

As kids, we probably all heard our parents say: "Don't eat so fast! Chew your food properly!" They may have added, "Don't talk while you're eating," and "Drink your milk carefully!" It's good advice for children — and for adults. Anyone can choke on food if he or she is not careful. That's why an important part of food service safety is being alert to your customers.

✕ Fast Fact

Approximately 4,000 people die annually from accidental choking in the United States.

Here's what to look for and what to do:

- If a person has both hands to the throat and cannot speak or cough, it is likely he or she is choking.

- If this person can talk, cough or breathe, do not pat him or her on the back or interfere in any way.

- If this person cannot talk, cough or breathe, you will need to take action. Use the Heimlich Maneuver, and call for help immediately.

You can also get a choke aide to demonstrate to employees. The Choke Aid Kit is an FDA-approved patented choke relieving device. It has a patented design with reach-extending handles and energy flex system, making it possible to save a choking victim safely and effectively. The device comes with a complete training kit, which includes a wall mount, booklet, poster and video that describes in detail how to save a choking victim with or without the device. Your establishment needs at least one of these kits in every workstation.

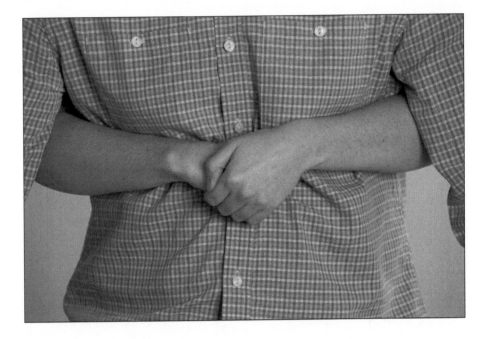

Exposure to Hazardous Chemicals

Improper exposure to cleaning agents, chemical pesticides and chemical sanitizers may cause injury to the skin or poisoning. To protect workers from exposure to hazardous materials, special precautions need to be taken, including certain steps that are required by law.

For example, the U.S. Department of Labor's OSHA requires food service establishments to keep a current inventory of all hazardous materials. Manufacturers are required to make sure hazardous chemicals are properly labeled and must supply a Material Safety Data Sheet (MSDS) to be kept on file at the food service facility. The MSDS provides the chemical name of the product and physical hazards, health hazards and emergency procedures in case of exposure.

Information about each chemical—including its common name, when it is used, who is authorized to use it, and information from the MSDS— must also be provided to workers.

To prevent improper exposure to hazardous materials, make sure:

- Only properly trained workers handle hazardous chemicals.

- Employees have safety equipment to use when working with hazardous chemicals.

- Employees wear nonporous gloves and eye goggles when working with sanitizing agents and other cleaners.

Employ the following steps when using hazardous chemicals:

1. Ask your supervisor any questions you may have about the substance.

2. Do not store chemicals near food storage, prep or serving areas.

3. Follow the directions on the label for proper handling, use and storage methods.

4. Do not leave aerosol cans near heat or spray near a source of flame.

5. Do not store chemicals in unmarked containers.

6. Know emergency procedures and who to call in case of an emergency.

7. Do not mix chemicals.

8. Read labels of all chemicals before using them.

9. Read how to properly dispose of empty containers before doing so.

10. Know where the Material Safety Data Sheets (MSDS) are posted and read them!

How to Read the MSDS:

There are six sections of the MSDS that provide you with safe-handling instructions:

1. Product name.

2. Whether the product is a fire hazard.

3. What health hazards occur if exposure or overexposure occurs.

4. Steps to follow in case of a spill.

5. Special protection needed when using the substance (gloves, goggles, etc.).

6. Special precautions to take when handling and storing.

Every restaurant employee is responsible for preparing and serving quality and safe food products. Each employee must be thoroughly familiar with basic food safety and sanitation practices. This chapter will describe the fundamental methods and procedures that must be practiced in order to control food contamination, the spread of infectious diseases, and personal safety practices.

Management must provide employees with the training, knowledge and tools that will enable them to establish and practice proper food handling and sanitation procedures. Through the use of this section, and under the guidance of your local department of health, you and your staff can obtain training and knowledge. First, however, the restaurant must be equipped with the proper tools, training and working conditions. Employees will never establish good sanitation procedures if they do not first have the proper environment in which to practice them.

Aside from what is required by law, the management should provide training materials, proper training sessions or clinics, hand sinks at every station, hand and nail brushes, labels for dating and rotation procedures, disposable towels, gloves, first-aid kits, germicidal hand soaps, employee restrooms and lockers, scrub brushes, uniforms, hairnets, thermometers, test kits, and quality, color-coded utensils.

Food service establishments may harbor all types of bacteria, bugs and animal pests. Restaurants can attract these health hazards with the three basic ingredients necessary to sustain life: food, water and warmth. Any environment that provides these three elements for an extended period of time will become host to these intruders. In order to eliminate contamination, all that is necessary is to make the living conditions unfavorable for these unwanted intruders.

 **Fast Fact**

Pest sightings can instantly ruin a restaurant's reputation. Surveys have shown that more than 60 percent of consumers would tell five or more acquaintances if they spotted pests in a restaurant, and 30 percent said that they would never return if they saw a roach.[14]

What is HACCP?

Hazard Analysis of Critical Control Points (HACCP) is a system for monitoring the food service process to reduce the risk of food-borne illness. HACCP focuses on how food flows through the process—from purchasing to serving. At each step in the food-preparation process there are a variety of potential hazards. HACCP provides managers with a framework for implementing control procedures for each hazard. It does this through

14. Siddiqi, 2008

identifying critical control points, or CCPs. These are points in the process where bacteria or other harmful organisms may grow or food may become contaminated.

Why use HACCP in your facility?

As a food service manager, you are responsible for protecting your customers by serving safe and wholesome food. To accomplish this, you have to educate your employees and motivate them to put into practice at every step what they've learned about food safety. To do this, you need a systematic process for identifying potential hazards, for putting safety procedures in place, and for monitoring the success of your safety system on an ongoing basis. HACCP helps you do all of these things.

Using HACCP, you can identify potentially hazardous foods and places in the food-preparation process where bacterial contamination, survival and growth can occur. Then you can take action to minimize the danger.

HACCP is based on this principle: If the raw ingredients are safe, and the process is safe, then the finished product is safe.

Implementing HACCP involves seven key steps. As you proceed through these steps, you will:

1. Assess the hazards.

2. Identify "critical control points."

3. Establish "critical limits."

4. Monitor the "critical control points."

5. Take corrective action as needed.

6. Develop a recordkeeping system.

7. Verify your system's effectiveness.

Avoid Bacterial Cross-Contamination

One of the most common causes of food-borne illness is cross-contamination: the transfer of bacteria from food to food, hand to food or equipment to food. While most cross-contamination cases occur in the back-of-the-house, servers can cause this situation, as well. An example of this is using the same cutting board to cut salad tomatoes and to slice raw chicken. Keep separate cutting boards for the salad and server areas. There are colored acrylic cutting boards on the market that can serve as a reminder for the board's use. Hang a sign up over the area the cutting boards are stored telling servers the green ones are for salad ingredients.

Food to food

Raw, contaminated ingredients may be added to foods, or fluids from raw foods may drip into foods that receive no further cooking. A common mistake is to leave thawing meat on a top shelf in the refrigerator where it can drip down onto prepared foods stored below.

Hand to food

Bacteria are found throughout the body: in the hair, on the skin, in clothing, in the mouth, nose and throat, in the intestinal tract, and on scabs or scars from skin wounds. These bacteria often end up on the hands where they can easily spread to food. People can also pick up bacteria by touching raw food, then transfer it to cooked or ready-to-eat food.

Equipment to food

Bacteria may pass from equipment to food when equipment that has touched contaminated food is then used to prepare other food without proper cleaning and sanitizing. For example, cross-contamination can occur when surfaces used for cutting raw poultry are then used to cut foods that will be eaten raw, such as fresh vegetables.

Coverings, such as plastic wrap and holding and serving containers, can also harbor bacteria that can spread to food. A can opener, a plastic-wrap box or a food slicer can also become a source of cross-contamination if not properly sanitized between uses.

Unsanitary practices

Unsanitary practices your servers should avoid include chewing gum, eating food in food-preparation areas and tasting food using their fingers. Also, make sure that servers cover any cuts, and use gloves when handling food. In addition, encourage your workers to stay home if they are ill. Someone with a cold or the flu should not be handling food. Restaurant workers are notorious for coming to work sick in order to avoid losing money. Encourage your employees to practice food safety by putting policies in place that will encourage them to stay home when ill. Consider providing your employees with sick time. Perhaps you could add it as a benefit after an employee has been with you for a certain length of time. By adding this benefit, you can keep your food supply safer and lower your turnover rate.

Danger zone

Keep foods out of the temperature danger zone (45 to 140 degrees Fahrenheit). Make sure to keep hot foods hot and cold foods cold.

Thawing foods

Thaw foods in the refrigerator, microwave, or under cold, running water. If using the running water method, do not leave foods out for more than 2 hours, and cook immediately upon thawing.

Reheating food

Do not use a steam table to reheat foods. Also be sure that when reheating, you bring the food's temperature up to 165 degrees Fahrenheit.

Cooling food

When cooling soups or stews, put it in several shallow pans so it will cool quickly. You can also use an ice bath to expedite the cooling process.

Using thermometers

If using an instant-read thermometer, be sure to place the stem into the food item so the dimple is covered. Also be sure thermometers are properly calibrated for using.

FIFO

Be sure to stress importance of "first in, first out" method of storage. This will ensure foods don't become outdated. Also be sure to label, date and cover all food items, and keep cleaning supplies in a separate storage area.

Online Information Resources

There are many food-safety information resources on the web. Check out the following sites for more information:

The Food Safety Preventive Controls Alliance at **www.ifsh.iit.edu/fspca** offers a variety of resources for those working in the food industry.

The USDA has training materials available on their website: **www.usda .gov/wps/portal/usda/usdahome?navid=food-nutrition.**

The Food Safety and Inspection Service of the United States Department of Agriculture has information and training resources. Check them out at **www.fsis.usda.gov/wps/portal/fsis/home.**

The American Food Safety's website at **www.americanfoodsafety.com** offers courses in food safety and Food Protection Manager Certification.

The FDA's "Bad Bug Book" offers up-to-date information on the major agents that cause foodborne illness. You can download it for free at **www.fda.gov/Food/FoodborneIllnessContaminants/CausesOfIllness BadBugBook.**

Food Handler provides temperature charts, signs, and free downloadable materials on food safety and industry applications at **http://handwashing forlife.com**. They also have videos that cover subjects like the importance of proper hygiene.

Other resources include Gateway to US Government Food Safety Information (**www.foodsafety.gov**) and The United States Department of Agriculture (**www.fns.usda.gov/food-safety/food-safety**).

Bacteria Primer

Bacteria are everywhere: in the air, in all areas of the restaurant, and all over one's body. Most bacteria are microscopic and of no harm to people. Many forms of bacteria are actually beneficial, aiding in the production of such things as cheese, bread, butter, alcoholic beverages, etc. Only a small percentage of bacteria will cause food to spoil and can generate a form of food poisoning when consumed.

Bacteria need food, water and warmth in order to survive. Their growth rate depends upon how favorable these conditions are. Bacteria prefer to ingest moisture-saturated foods, such as meats, dairy products and produce. They will not grow as readily on dry foods such as cereals, sugar or flour.

Bacteria will grow most rapidly when the temperature is between 85–100 degrees Fahrenheit. In most cases, the growth rate will slow down drastically if the temperature is hotter or colder than this. Thus, it is vitally important that perishable food items are refrigerated before bacteria have a chance to establish themselves and multiply. Certain bacteria can survive in extreme hot- and cold-temperature ranges. By placing these bacteria in severe temperatures you will be slowing down their growth rate, but not necessarily killing them.

 *Fast Fact*

The greatest problem in controlling bacteria is their rapid reproduction cycle. Approximately every 15 minutes the bacteria count will double under optimal living conditions.

The more bacteria present, the greater the chance of bacterial infection. This is why food products that must be subjected to conditions favorable to bacteria are done so for the shortest period possible.

An important consideration when handling food products is that bacteria need several hours to adjust to a new environment before they are able to begin rapidly multiplying. Thus, if you had removed a food product from the walk-in refrigerator and had inadvertently introduced bacteria to it, advanced growth would not begin for several hours. If you had immediately placed the item back into the walk-in, the temperature would have killed the bacteria before it became established.

Bacterial forms do not have a means of transportation; they must be introduced to an area by some other vehicle. People are primarily responsible for transporting bacteria to new areas. The body temperature of 98.6 degrees Fahrenheit is perfect for bacterial existence and proliferation. A person coughing, sneezing or wiping their hands on a counter can introduce bacteria to an area. Bacteria may be transmitted also by insects, air, water and articles onto which they have attached themselves, such as boxes, blades, knives and cutting boards.

Dangerous Forms of Bacteria

The following section describes a number of harmful bacteria that may be found in a restaurant. The technical names and jargon are given for your own information. The important points to retain are the causes and preventive actions for each.

Clostridium perfringens

Clostridium perfringens is one of a group of bacterial infectious diseases that will cause a poisoning effect. These bacteria are extremely dangerous because they are tasteless, odorless and colorless, and therefore nearly impossible to detect.

Clostridium perfringens are usually found in meat or seafood that was previously cooked and then held at room temperature for a period of time. These perfringens are anaerobic. They do not need air in order to survive. They can thrive in masses of food or in canned foods in the form of botulism. In order to survive, the bacterium will form a spore and surround itself. The spore will protect the bacterium from exposure to the air and give it a much wider temperature range for survival than normal bacteria: 65–120 degrees Fahrenheit. These bacterial forms may survive through long periods of extreme temperature and then multiply when the conditions are more favorable.

Keeping cooked food consistently above 148 degrees Fahrenheit or below 40 degrees Fahrenheit eliminates clostridium perfringens bacteria.

Clostridium botulism

This is another of the poisoning forms of bacteria. Botulism is a rare infectious disease but it is far more lethal than the other types. Botulism exists only in an air-free environment like that of canned goods. These bacteria are most often found in home-canned goods; however, several national food packers have reported outbreaks in their operations.

Symptoms such as vomiting, double vision, abdominal pain and shock may occur anytime from three to four hours after ingestion to eight days later. Examine all canned goods closely before using. Look for dented, leaking cans and swollen cans or jar tops.

Staphylococci poisoning

Staphylococci bacteria (Staph) are perhaps the most common cause of food poisoning. Staph bacteria can be found everywhere, particularly in the human nose. The bacteria by themselves are harmless. The problem arises when they are left uncontrolled to grow in food items. Food that has been left out, unrefrigerated, for just a few hours can produce the poisonous toxins of Staph bacteria.

Symptoms will appear two to six hours after consumption. Common symptoms are vomiting, muscle weakness, cramps and diarrhea. The sickness ranges from very severe cases — sometimes lethal — to a relatively mild illness.

 **Fast Fact**

Prevent Staph poisoning by following refrigeration procedures precisely. Only remove the refrigerated food items that you will be using right away.

Salmonella infection

Salmonella infection is directly caused by the bacteria themselves, after consumption by a human.

In certain cases, death has resulted; however, usually Salmonella cause severe, but temporary, illness. Symptoms are vomiting, fever, abdominal pain and cramps. Symptoms usually show up 12–24 hours after consumption and may last for several days.

Salmonella are found in the intestinal tract of some animals. They have been discovered in some packaged foods, eggs, poultry, seafood and meat. Thorough cooking and following refrigeration procedures can keep Salmonella growth to a safe limit.

Hepatitis, Dysentery and Diphtheria are some of the other infectious diseases that are bacterially derived.

Controlling Bacteria

The first step in controlling bacteria is to limit their access to the restaurant. Make certain that all products entering the restaurant are clean. Follow the prescribed bug-exterminating procedures to stop bacteria from being transported into the restaurant. Keep all food products stored and refrigerated as prescribed. Clean up any spills as you go along, making the environment unsuitable for bacteria to live. Keep all food refrigerated until needed, and cook it as soon as possible.

The quality known as "pH" indicates how acidic or alkaline ("basic") a food or other substance is. The pH scale ranges from 0.0 to 14.0—7.0 being exactly neutral. Distilled water, for example, has a neutral pH of 7.0. Bacteria grow best in foods that are neutral or slightly acidic, in the pH range of 4.6 to 7.0. Highly acidic foods, such as vinegar and most fresh fruits, inhibit bacterial growth. Meats and many other foods have an optimal pH for bacterial growth. On the other hand, some foods normally considered hazardous, such as mayonnaise and custard filling, can be safely stored at room temperature if their pH is below 4.6.

Lowering the pH of foods by adding acidic ingredients, such as making sauerkraut from cabbage or pickles from cucumbers, may render them non-potentially hazardous. This is not a foolproof prevention method, however. For example, although commercially prepared mayonnaise has a pH below 4.6, adding mayonnaise to a meat salad will not inhibit bacteria. The moisture in the meat and the meat's pH are likely to raise the pH of the salad to a point where bacteria can multiply.

Hygiene

Personal hygiene is the best way to stop bacteria from contaminating and spreading into new areas. Hands are the greatest source of contamination. Hands must be washed constantly throughout the day. Every time an individual scratches her head or sneezes, she is exposing her hands to bacteria and will spread it to anything she touches, such as food, equipment and clothes. Hand and nail brushes, antibacterial soaps and disposable gloves should be a part of every restaurant, even if not required by law. Proper training and management follow-up is also critical.

Every employee must practice good basic hygiene:

- Short hair, and/or hair contained in a net.

- Clean-shaven, or facial hair contained in a net.

- Clean clothes/uniforms.

- Clean hands and short nails.

- No unnecessary jewelry.

- A daily shower or bath.

- No smoking in or near the kitchen.

- Hand-washing, prior to starting work, periodically, and after handling any foreign object: head, face, ears, money, food, boxes or trash.

 *Fast Fact*

An employee who has the symptoms of the common cold or any open cuts or infections should not go to work. By simply breathing, he or she may be inadvertently exposing the environment to bacteria.

Although it is rarely practiced in the food industry, all employees should be required to have a complete medical examination as a condition of employment. This should include blood and urine tests. A seemingly healthy individual may unknowingly be the carrier of a latent communicable disease.

Hand-washing is perhaps the most critical aspect of good personal hygiene in food service. Employees should wash their hands after the following activities:

- Smoking (hands come in contact with mouth).

- Eating (hands come in contact with mouth).

- Using the restroom.

- Handling money.

- Touching raw food (the raw food may contain bacteria).

- Touching or combing their hair.

- Coughing, sneezing or blowing their nose.

- Taking a break.

- Handling anything dirty (touching a dirty apron or taking out the trash, for example).

Workers should wash their hands with soap and warm water for 20 seconds. When working with food, they should wash gloved hands as often as bare hands. The proper hand-washing method is as follows:

1. Remove any jewelry.

2. Turn water on as hot as you can stand it.

3. Moisten hands and forearms up to elbows.

4. Lather them thoroughly with soap.

5. Wash for at least 20 seconds, rubbing hands together, washing between fingers and up to the elbows.

6. Use a brush for under nails.

7. Rinse hands and forearms with hot water.

8. Dry hands and forearms with a paper towel.

When handling tableware, you should:

- Use plastic gloves if directly handling gloves (remember, just because you have a glove on does not mean you can't cross-contaminate).

- Use plastic scoops in the ice machine.

- Avoid touching food contact surfaces. For instance, servers should not carry glasses by the rim and they should carry plates by the bottom or edge, keeping their hands away from eating surfaces. Employees should also pick up silverware by the handles.

Conclusion

Working in the restaurant industry can be hard and stressful, but it can also be emotionally and financially rewarding when your customers have had a good experience. Food, location, and atmosphere have a lot to do with what makes a restaurant great; But without a sharp and well-trained waitstaff, these things can't stand on their own.

Results from Zagat's "State of American Dining 2016" survey indicate just how important a restaurant's waitstaff can be to customers. When asked about bad dining experiences, the No. 1 complaint among participants was poor service—easily beating noise, prices, and crowds. Clearly, when it comes to customer satisfaction, waitstaff training is one of the best investments your restaurant can make. Not only does it boost customer satisfaction and sales, but it also improves your employees' work environment and helps make your restaurant the best that it can be.

Glossary

A la carte: Food items that are ordered and priced separately, unlike a set meal

Appetizer: A small portion of food or drink taken before a meal in order to stimulate the appetite

Arm service: When a server delivers meals by hand without aid of a tray or cart

Atmosphere: The sound, sight, smell, and overall feel of a location

Blood alcohol concentration: The concentration of alcohol in the bloodstream displayed as a percentage

Boning: The process of taking the bones out of meat or fish

Buffet: A meal with several dishes from which customers can pick and choose

Bussing: Clearing and cleaning a table after a customer's meal

Canapés: A tiny piece of pastry or bread with a topped with savory food

Clostridium Perfringens: A bacterium often found in the intestines of animals and on raw meat and poultry

CPR: Cardiopulmonary resuscitation, a life-saving emergency procedure that is performed when someone has stopped breathing or their heart has stopped

Critical control points: Specific food manufacturing procedures or steps where control can help reduce the possibility of food safety hazards

Cross-Contamination: When harmful bacteria or similar microorganisms are transferred from one object or substance to another

Daiquiri: A cocktail consisting of lime juice and rum

Entrée: A meal's main course

Expediter: A server whose main job is to increase efficiency by delivering food to tables

Expenditure: The amount spent

Fine Dining: A restaurant experience with a formal atmosphere and high-quality food that caters to upscale customers

Flambé: Food covered with liquor and set on fire

Food Poisoning: Sickness caused by consuming spoiled food

Garnish: Decoration on a plate or drink

Head Waiter: The person in charge of a restaurant's waitstaff

Hors d'oeuvres: A small dish or portion of food

Host/Hostess: The person in charge of welcoming and seating guests in a restaurant

IRS: The Internal Revenue Service

Liability: Being under obligation or debt

Maitre d': The person in charge of the dining room service

Menu: List of dishes served at a restaurant

Portion: A specific amount of something

Strain: An injury generally caused by overexertion or misuse of a muscle

Voucher: A piece of paper that entitles the holder to a discount

Wages: The amount of money received or paid for work

Wine Steward: The waiter who serves and helps patrons choose wine

Bibliography

"2016 Restaurant Industry Pocket Factbook." *National Restaurant Organization.* 2016. Web. 1 Nov. 2016.

C, Kalpana. "Tipping in Restaurants | SurveyMonkey Blog." *SurveyMonkey.* 18 Apr. 2013. Web. 02 Nov. 2016.

Knapton, Sarah. "The Most Stressful Job? Waitressing, Say Scientists." *The Telegraph.* Telegraph Media Group, 14 Oct. 2015. Web. 31 Oct. 2016.

Lawrence, Kevin. "How to Profit from Customer Complaints." *Coach Kevin Kevin.* 14 June 2006. Web. 02 Nov. 2016.

Morley, Miranda. "Revenue That Comes With Selling Alcohol." *Small Business.* Web. 02 Nov. 2016.

"Restaurant Technology Survey 2016." *National Restaurant Organization.* 2016. Web. 2 Nov. 2016.

Siddiqi, Zia. "Keep Your Restaurant's Reputation Pest-Free." *Foodservice.com.* Food Service, 16 Apr. 2008. Web. 02 Nov. 2016.

"Study Finds Americans Reluctant to Dine at Restaurants Where a Slip-and-Fall Accident Occurred." *Business Wire.* Berkshire Hathaway, 7 Mar. 2012. Web. 31 Oct. 2016.

"The State of American Dining in 2016." *Zagat.* 26 Jan. 2016. Web. 02 Nov. 2016.

Index

A la carte: 44, 126, 129, 273

Abbreviations: 97, 112, 177, 185

Atmosphere: 142, 143, 227, 271, 273, 274

Accidents: 10, 29, 33, 162, 163, 247, 248

Advertising: 153

Alcohol: 9, 22, 36, 158, 159, 197-203, 210, 213, 217, 220, 273, 275

Allergies: 24, 112, 138

American service: 6, 62, 66

Approach: 101, 103, 111, 154

Arm service: 7, 121, 273

Arrangements: 5, 54-56, 137, 190

Attention: 6, 28, 34, 51, 97, 103, 111, 131, 135, 146, 154, 156, 157, 175

Attitude: 34, 48, 85, 102, 105

Attorney: 189, 190

Bacteria: 10, 256-259, 261-269, 274

Bacteria Primer: 10, 261

Bank: 180, 183, 184

Bar: 9, 36, 160, 173, 174, 183, 192, 203, 210, 214, 225-229, 235-238, 242

Bartender: 203, 210, 211, 226, 228, 236, 241, 242

Beer: 10, 79, 197, 207-209, 230-235, 238

Behavior: 161

Benefits: 174, 192, 194

Beverage: 1, 2, 9, 37, 64, 84, 88, 109, 111, 114, 115, 117, 125, 129, 131, 134, 190, 191, 197, 210, 211

Blood alcohol concentration: 199, 273

Boning: 69, 71, 273

Booster seats: 146, 244

Booth: 85

Bottle: 9, 70, 112, 135, 210, 213-215, 222-230

Bourbon: 202-204

Brandy: 203, 206, 207, 238

Bread: 8, 25, 31, 44, 50, 57, 77, 84, 87, 88, 101, 113, 128, 131, 137, 153, 168, 261, 273

Bread baskets: 8, 25, 153
Break: 21, 22, 24, 25, 32, 46,
    184, 231, 269
Breakfast: 76-78, 85-87, 89
Buffet: 6, 65, 94, 273
Buffet service: 6, 65
Bus Person: 24, 38, 50, 114, 243,
    244
Bussing: 7, 10, 23, 121, 243, 273
Butter: 44, 50, 71, 73, 77, 79, 83,
    85, 87, 91, 101, 113, 114, 136,
    151, 153, 168, 174, 261

Canapés: 90, 273
Captain: 36, 37, 59
Carbons: 179
Carving: 69, 72
Cash: 24, 113, 118, 171, 173-
    175, 179, 181, 183, 184, 191-
    194, 196
Cash register: 24, 113, 171, 173,
    181, 183
Cashier: 8, 176, 178, 179,
    181-184
CCPs: 257
Cellphone: 161
Centerpieces: 6, 92, 94, 95, 244
Champagne: 202, 213, 219, 222,
    224, 225
Checklist: 22
Cheese: 85, 138, 168, 186, 219,
    261
Chef: 114, 130, 237
Children: 50, 59, 103, 105, 111,
    116, 136, 143, 144, 147, 244,
    252

China: 19, 36, 73, 74, 79, 84, 92,
    108
Choke Aid Kit: 252
Choking: 10, 252
Choosing: 17, 135, 222
Cleaning: 23, 25, 29, 157, 162,
    244, 253, 259, 260, 273
Clearing: 7, 23, 67, 106, 109,
    116, 245, 273
Clerical work: 5, 54
Closing: 23, 25, 37, 155, 233
Clostridium Perfringens: 264, 273
Coffee: 8, 23, 25, 39, 44, 50, 57,
    64, 67, 73, 81, 84-87, 89, 91,
    98, 101, 109, 114-117, 120,
    125, 136, 152, 211, 235, 236,
    238
Coffee service: 8, 64, 87, 109,
    117, 152
Cognac: 206, 207
Competition: 171
Complaints: 8, 37, 43, 48, 52,
    54, 153, 154, 156, 158, 275
Complimentary food: 182
Computer: 27, 173, 184, 187
Cook: 21, 65, 69, 71, 185, 260,
    266
Cooking: 8, 69-71, 167-169, 177,
    181, 258, 266
Cooling: 260
Cover: 64, 70, 74-81, 84, 86-92,
    101, 106, 113, 259-261
CPR: 248, 273
Crayons: 144
Credit: 24, 31, 107, 118, 175,
    178-180, 192, 224

Credit cards: 31, 175
Critical control points: 256, 257, 273
Criticism: 47, 48
Cross-Contamination: 10, 258, 259, 274

Daiquiries: 240, 241
Decoration: 274
Dessert: 7, 23, 32, 51, 67, 77, 78, 81, 84, 89, 91, 98, 106, 109, 116, 117, 125, 126, 129-132, 157, 218, 219
Difficult customers: 8, 155
Dinner: 62, 64, 75, 76, 78-81, 89, 90, 92, 94, 101, 106, 113, 115, 116, 120, 125, 128, 131, 137, 139, 184, 212, 213, 218
Disabled: 58, 137

Efficiency: 14, 38, 42, 52, 171, 274
Electronic ordering: 8, 172, 175
Email: 2, 140
EmTRAC: 190-192
English service: 6, 64
Entertainers: 45
Entrées: 24, 67, 116, 120, 212
Expediter: 28, 99, 181, 274

Facebook: 27
Falling: 10, 250
Family: 35, 36, 64, 143, 145-147
Family: 35, 36, 64, 143, 145-147
Family-Style Service: 66
Fine Dining: 35, 36, 68, 274

Fire: 10, 71, 240, 248, 251, 255, 274
Fire Department: 10, 240, 248, 251
Fire extinguisher: 71, 248, 251
First aid: 248
Fish: 57, 69, 71, 144, 218, 273
Flambé: 69, 70, 274
Food Poisoning: 163, 261, 265, 274
Forks: 76-78, 84, 86-88, 90, 116
Fraud: 179
French Service: 6, 62-64
Fruit: 84, 86, 87, 91, 125, 128, 129, 169, 207, 211, 219, 221, 236, 240, 241

Garnishes: 10, 111, 114, 211, 230, 236, 237
General manager: 36, 37
Gin: 32, 104, 203, 206
Glassware: 9, 44, 73, 74, 79, 84, 92, 202, 222, 232, 233, 240, 245
Gloves: 254-256, 259, 267, 270
Gratitude: 32

HACCP: 10, 256, 257
Hazard Analysis of Critical Control Points: 256
Hazardous: 10, 253, 254, 257, 267
Head Waiter: 37, 274
High chairs: 146, 244
Hiring: 17, 21, 33, 36
Hors d'oeuvres: 90, 274

Hostess: 5, 27, 37, 38, 41-43, 46-51, 64, 87, 103, 110, 114, 126, 201, 274

Hours: 18, 27, 28, 30, 31, 36, 43, 45, 54, 64, 149, 260, 263, 265

House: 32, 140, 159, 203, 212, 214, 241

Housed food: 183

Hygiene: 11, 23-25, 261, 267, 269

Ice: 44, 64, 73, 82, 83, 91, 126, 128, 151, 210, 222, 228, 229, 236, 238, 240, 260, 270

Ice cream: 44, 64, 91, 126, 128

Illness: 256, 258, 261, 265

Internet: 2, 175

Intoxication: 198-200

IRS: 189-192, 194-196, 274

Juice: 84, 86, 128, 166, 206, 211, 229, 236, 274

Kids: 7, 8, 143-147, 252

Knives: 76-78, 115, 263

Lawsuit: 198

Liability: 2, 158, 197, 274

License: 197

Linen: 44, 51, 54, 73, 74, 85, 109, 117

Liquor: 70, 79, 181, 197, 203, 205, 207, 210, 225-229, 240, 274

Loading: 7, 115, 120, 249

Lobby: 37, 139, 161, 244

Loyal: 46, 47

Lunch: 29, 87, 89, 103

Maitre d': 37, 274

Manager: 2, 15, 29, 32, 36, 37, 42, 46, 52, 54, 99, 114, 126, 130, 134, 140, 154, 157-160, 163, 174, 176, 180, 182-184, 187, 198, 201, 214, 224, 244, 257, 261

Manager food: 182

Material Safety Data Sheet: 253

Meat: 57, 69, 71-73, 77, 79, 87, 98, 112, 125, 126, 128, 130, 169, 247, 258, 264, 266, 267, 273

Menu cards: 44, 49

Money: 8, 55, 57, 108, 171, 174, 175, 180, 183, 189, 195, 236, 259, 268, 269, 274

Napkins: 6, 23, 49, 76, 81, 92, 93, 104, 112, 136, 150, 242

National Restaurant Association: 144, 171, 173

Online: 10, 27, 137, 140, 145, 171, 175, 216, 260

Pests: 256

Pets: 160

Phone: 2, 37, 56, 140, 158, 180

Phraseology: 132

Portion: 227, 273, 274

POS: 27, 172-175, 178, 181

Pouring: 10, 215, 224-232, 238, 241
Problems: 8, 10, 15, 30, 32, 158, 180, 198, 233
Proof: 204-206, 210

Quality: 10, 37, 38, 63, 132, 133, 204, 206, 217, 221, 231, 235-237, 240, 255, 256, 267

Raw food: 259, 269
Receipt: 118, 177, 178, 181, 183, 184
Red Cross: 10, 248
Reheating: 260
Reporting: 190-193, 195, 196
Reservation: 54-56
Restroom: 147, 269
Roach: 256
Rowdy tables: 160
Rum: 203, 206, 274
Russian Service: 6, 65, 90

Safety: 9, 10, 15, 199, 247, 248, 252-255, 257, 259, 261, 273
Salad: 19, 62, 63, 65, 70, 78-80, 84, 88, 90, 98, 109, 112, 117, 124, 125, 127, 129, 130, 156, 169, 186, 258, 267
Salmonella: 265, 266
Sanitation: 10, 38, 247, 255, 256
Satisfaction: 19, 30, 38, 42, 52, 131, 272
Scotch: 136, 202, 203, 205, 210, 213

Shorthand: 28, 185
Shot: 210, 226-230
Silver: 44, 63, 73, 74, 76, 77, 83, 84, 88-91, 152, 245
Silverware: 25, 74, 76, 83, 84, 92, 141, 245, 270
Single malt: 205
Slipping: 10, 249, 250
Smartphone: 171, 172, 214
Smoking: 268, 269
Social media: 27, 140
Soda: 91, 203, 213, 226, 232
Soup: 30, 62, 67, 84, 88, 90, 91, 101, 113, 126, 128-130, 137, 156, 167, 170, 219
Specials: 8, 15, 27, 37, 38, 104, 105, 111, 112, 123, 124, 130, 145
Spoons: 67, 77, 78, 84, 87, 91
Staphylococci Poisoning: 265
Strain: 19, 250, 274
Substitutions: 7, 44, 51, 113, 126, 138
Suggesting: 7, 124, 129, 131, 132, 169
Suggestive selling: 7, 23, 123, 126, 127, 129, 133, 135

Table d'hôte: 43, 125
Tables: 7, 13, 23, 25, 33, 37-39, 41, 43, 49-51, 54, 56, 58, 59, 63, 71, 73, 74, 79, 92, 110, 137, 147, 160, 176, 243-245, 249, 274
Tableware: 109, 117, 270

Tasting: 9, 68, 130, 216, 219, 220, 259

Technology: 8, 14, 171, 172, 175, 177, 275

Tequila: 203, 207

Thermometer: 260

Tickets: 8, 57, 181-184

Timing: 100, 124, 131

Tipping: 22, 107, 190, 275

Tips: 7, 9, 30, 32, 33, 111, 133, 139, 141, 189, 191-197, 219, 232

Tossing: 69, 70

Touch screen: 173

TRAC: 190-192, 195

Training: 1, 2, 13-15, 21, 22, 36, 42, 62, 97, 119, 199, 213, 225, 248, 252, 255, 256, 261, 267, 272

Trays: 7, 23, 25, 33, 63, 64, 82, 84, 119-121, 139, 151, 244, 249

TRDA: 190-192, 195

Turnover: 13, 259

Twitter: 27

Unsanitary practices: 259

Up-selling: 32

Vermouth: 207, 208

Vodka: 104, 203, 205

Voucher: 179, 274

Wages: 19, 196, 274

Website: 2, 27, 68, 140, 192, 196, 216, 261

Well items: 203, 226

Whipped cream: 10, 235, 236

Whiskey: 202-205

Whisky: 205

Wine: 9, 15, 23, 36-38, 68, 79, 112, 133, 135, 174, 181, 183, 197, 202, 207, 208, 212-217, 219-225, 236, 274

Wine Steward: 36, 37, 274